A DREAMER'S APOLOGY

A Collection of Thoughts, Observations and Experiences

Tan Boon Tee PhD

ATHENA PRESS
LONDON

A DREAMER'S APOLOGY
A Collection of Thoughts, Observations and Experiences
Copyright © Tan Boon Tee PhD 2003

ISBN 1 84401 132 1

First Published 2003 by
ATHENA PRESS
Queen's House, 2 Holly Road
Twickenham TW1 4EG
United Kingdom

Printed for Athena Press

A DREAMER'S APOLOGY
A Collection of Thoughts, Observations and Experiences

*Dedicated to my family and those who have in one way or
another shared my life.*

Foreword

One of the pleasures of the editor's occupation, is that when you open a manuscript, you are launching the vessel of understanding onto an unknown sea; you cannot know what to expect; often you are disappointed, but occasionally one finds something of value and interest.

This is such a case. This is not a book to read at a sitting. It is a mellowed, reflective volume of personal philosophy, elegantly expressed; it is a volume in which to dip, to wander, and to think on.

Every page has some observation which, while the point may have been made before by others, is invariably given a slant of originality. The author is never trite and never predictable.

At this moment, the UK is embroiled in a discussion about the costs of higher education. Dr Tan has just the words for this controversy:

> *'If you think education is expensive, try ignorance, or better still, try illiteracy.'*

Bang. Makes the point like a gunshot.

This volume is chock-a-block with gems such as this.

Mark Sykes
London

About the Author

Dr Tan Boon Tee has been a science and mathematics teacher, curriculum developer, school principal and educator for the past thirty-six years in Southeast Asia. A former university senior lecturer, he served as a UNESCO regional consultant in science education during the 1980s.

Dr Tan's main area of research interest is in students' conceptual framework and cognitive impediment in physics. Some two dozen of his papers have been presented in various international conferences, seminars and symposiums in eighteen countries across the continents since 1977.

He is married and has seven children, one grandchild.

Contents

A Word or Two

This is part of the collection of my thoughts, observations, insights and experiences over the past decade. It covers a wide area of human life and activities.

To maximise the impact of the precepts, you as readers are requested to go through each of them slowly and at your own pace. Most of them are meant to be digested, assimilated, and absorbed into your own perceptions, knowledge, and wisdom, while others are to be taken with a light heart.

I can only claim 80% ownership of the originality, the remaining 20% may resemble aphorisms from a myriad of other sources.

It is not my intention to offend any particular person, gender or profession, and readers are entitled to their own opinions and thinking. I believe a good number of elderly people will have had quite similar life experiences.

Enjoy your reading.

Tan Boon Tee
March 2003

A Matter of Perception

We may escape from being imprisoned for the vices we committed, but the vices will keep haunting us and 'imprison' us for the rest of our lives.

Vanity cuts across gender. It is a curved mirror that gives us illusions of glory.

Holidaying in remote places appears to be attractive in advertisement. It is like making an acquaintance with a pretty girl: you never know where the hidden danger lies.

Many people going on holiday overseas do not really want to go seeing new places or experiencing different cultures. The important thing is to tell others when they return that they were 'there'.

Utopia, like heaven, is a concept; it is to be believed but not to be trusted.

If a friend is envious of your success, he is not your true friend.

Envy is a highly contagious virus, it spreads far and wide.

When is enough enough? There is no possible answer for this, as everyone has his own set of criteria.

Ecstasy and agony are close identical twins, you cannot have one without the other.

Why do we like to hear about others' suffering or misfortune? Surely we do not enjoy hearing it – or it is because it makes us feel that we are better off?

English is incomprehensible. When it is right, it is not wrong; but when it is left, it must not be right.

English is still incomprehensible. The word 'likable' is 'able' added to 'like' with the 'e' dropped. The word 'chargeable' is 'able' added to 'charge' with the 'e' retained. Similarly, able added to size is 'sizeable', but it can also be 'sizable', which happens to have a slightly different meaning.

This world thrives with all kinds of energy source. In fact, without energy all things are dead.

We survive on energy. Has anyone thought about what would happen to us when all available sources of energy have been depleted (bearing in mind that the sun's radiation energy may easily be blocked by nuclear fallout particles)?

The difference between life and death is that there is no difference.

Give me dignity or give me death – liberty comes after dignity.

A diplomat will smile at you even if he is angry.

Diplomacy is a skill, the verbal skill of saying 'maybe', 'perhaps', 'possibly' and 'probably', instead of a firm 'yes' or 'no'.

Diplomacy is the art of saying things you do not quite know and keeping silent about things you know.

Diplomacy is the sum of partying and partying added to chatting and chatting.

In any conversation, you can agree to disagree; but it will be very difficult for you to disagree and still remain agreeable.

During the cold war, the superpowers kept inventing super-weapons to balance the power equation. After the cold war, the only superpower continues to build ultra-weapons to keep its superiority.

Now the arms race has stopped, leaving only a sole runner who does not seem keen to stop. The only outcome is that the human race will eventually stop.

Now that the cost of medical treatment and medicine is so exorbitant, I dread falling sick, especially after retirement.

Ask a person, 'Are you really honest?' If he answers, 'Yes, of course I am honest', chances are he is not that honest after all.

The path of least resistance is not necessarily straight; at least for the river, it isn't – and neither for man too.

The worst disillusion one can have is that after decades of marriage, one finds that it was not the right marriage at the very beginning.

There are things you do not like to do, but you have to do. There are also things you do not have to do, but you like to do.

If you do not do anything you don't like, probably you are not doing anything at all.

Anything Else?

There are many types of vitamins which help to keep us healthy. We need at least four more: Vitamin G for eliminating greed, J for jealousy, R for rage and V for vanity.

Do not jump into conclusions, all you get will be confusions.

Genes make us what we are – thanks to genes, no thanks to genes.

Most of us tend to associate things which have no causal relationship whatsoever. This results in unnecessary complications of all kinds.

You are what you eat; you are also what you do not eat.

We are judged by the company we keep; we are also judged by the company we do not keep.

To many women, their children are more important than their husbands – they can leave their husbands but not their children.

The law sometimes has its way – to prove the guilty innocent, and the innocent guilty.

To a certain extent, we have to be a little insane to survive in this mad world.

The world may just happen to be a huge mental asylum in our universe.

To mad people, the sane person is the mad one.

He says he is only sincere when he says he is not sincere. Is he really sincere?

Is inspiration a mixture of insipidity and reason? If not, why are only so few people inspired?

If you cannot laugh an insult off, you probably deserve it.

When people call themselves intellectuals, most likely they do not have that much intelligence per se.

There is no such thing as average intelligence. Either you are intelligent or you are not.

The first person required to take an intelligence test ought to be the leader of the country.

Intelligence comes in different forms. So there are many types of intelligent people.

Beware of showing your good intentions. They can easily turn sour overnight.

How often is a person interested in things around him other than himself?

What you say may not be what is interpreted. This is one of the main causes of friction.

Interruption is rude and inconsiderate, especially to a sensitive speaker.

All of us have intuition, though some are better at it than others; but none can beat a suspicious married woman.

The greatest invention is the invention of how to go about inventing.

Necessity is the mother of invention. This may not be true anymore; it is the other way round now.

Only people in love will equate jealousy to love. Jealousy is the worst form of selfishness.

A man with a split personality is one whose right hand does not know what the left hand is doing.

A spendthrift does not know how to spend his money right, and ends up with nothing left.

The pursuit of happiness at 150 km per hour can only bring one eternal peace.

Like a lady's skirt, an interesting speech is one which is long enough to cover the object yet short enough to arouse curiosity.

A precise speech that goes right to the point is worth more than ten long-winded and pointless speeches.

Is it not that opinions are often wild speculations in disguise?

Scientists are still searching for extraterrestrial intelligent beings. Have they already given up hope in looking for one on earth?

What is the use of having a conscience without a soul?

A simple cure for any grief is to tell it to as many people as possible.

The trouble with some of us is the trying too hard to be sophisticated when we just cannot be sophisticated.

Life is like a song. There are as many different lives as there are songs.

If you have a phobia of being alone, do not try solitude.

A casual visit to solitude is fine, but a long indulgence in it can lead to madness.

The more I learn, the less I know. The less I know, the more I want to learn – the end result is I know less and less.

There are mainly five types of people in a society: informers, conformers, non-informers, reformers and non-conformers.

To the drunks, a sober person is the only one intoxicated – sort of.

A snob always thinks he is a notch above the others. Fortunately, he only thinks he is.

The most beautiful curve on a human body is the smile.

A smile can perform wonders; even an infant can detect it.

Put on a smile, it costs you nothing and yet relaxes your facial muscles too.

Never stick your nose into other people's business, it smells.

Try and give time some time to settle down; there's no need to be too hasty in everything.

There's nothing wrong in making a slip or two, except of course on the wrong occasion.

Sleep is a gentle mediator. It mediates between two dreary working days.

A true sceptic is someone who neither believes what he says nor what anyone else says – in fact he does not believe in anything at all.

One of the most embarrassing moments is when a speaker means what he said to be a joke and the audience is in complete silence.

One man's joke can turn out to be another man's insult.

If you want your private life history to be exposed, run for a presidency – of any kind.

If you want to be popular or famous, employ a journalist.

Journalism takes on things usually left over by literature.

Only the impartial people are fit to be in a jury. But then how many of us are truly impartial?

Justice is a beautiful word, yet it's often abused. In the name of justice, how many injustices have been committed?

Juvenile delinquency seems to increase as society progresses. This is really painful to many a parent.

Juvenile delinquents nowadays are not as innocent as you may like to think. They are certainly not oblivious of the harm they will cause to their parents.

The milk of human kindness is often condensed, if

not evaporated.

Pity the know-alls, for they do not know what they are doing.

How do you fancy that? Private sin is no sin, only public sin is.

Things may not be as complex as they appear. Give them a try and they may become simple.

Like temptation, sin comes in all disguises – you are your own saviour.

The whole is not just greater than the sum of the parts, it is simpler too.

There is a time to talk, there is also a time to be reticent.

Silence can be golden, but prolonged silence under oppression is cowardice.

Silence is indeed golden, there's so little of it.

One's reticence can well be the source of another's curiosity.

No other highway signboard can be as effective as 'Police'.

When you cannot see clearly, you go to an optician. When you cannot think clearly, whom do you see?

Beware of love at first sight. It is the prelude to hate at last sight.

Some of us do not mind persons, we are just sick of people (at least some people).

For complacent people, a shock or two would do marvels.

On the other hand, if you are constantly bombarded by shocks, you are a dead duck.

A little knowledge is dangerous, but a lot of ignorance is more dangerous.

A successful life consists of four knows: know-how, know-when, know-what, and most important of all, know-whom.

Somebody knows what nobody knows, but nobody knows what everybody knows.

Learning without actually knowing what is being learnt is just like having a library of unused books in the basement.

Many an area of study is not quite precise and exact. Language is the worst.

Are You Sure?

Do not look at any obituary – only the good people are dead.

Why be so uptight? After all, an obituary is the last good thing said about a person.

Nothing is objectionable, as long as the insult is not directed at oneself.

Is there any point in telling the truth in the court? Chances are all you get is an objection from the lawyer.

Nothing is more objectionable than seeing a liar trying to hide his lie by making up more and more lies.

If you do not catch your obsession early and get rid of it, it will get in you in no time – the consequence is madness.

A life without any obstacles? You must be joking.

A life without any hurdles to cross? What a dry and dull life it is!

Obstacles may well be the right stepping stones to your achievement – the greater the obstacles, the greater the achievement.

The world is full of nobody, somebody and everybody. Everybody wants to get a job done, somebody has to do it, but nobody knows who.

It is all right to grow old – it's just that one is not young any more.

The older one becomes, the shorter one's future is.

Surgical operations are very common nowadays. They are so common that few of us would want to brag about our experiences.

To be in agreement with someone's opinion sometimes is a gentle form of flattery. But to be supportive of someone's opinions all the time is lowly.

The word 'everybody' has been grossly abused, unfortunately. When someone says, 'Everybody does it', he implies many other people are doing it, while in actual fact he is the only one doing it.

Opinions are not facts, albeit they tend to sound factual. More often than not, they are just prejudices and biases in disguise.

Where opportunities are rare, opportunists multiply.

Never look for an opportunity lost, you will be surprised how fast someone else has picked it up.

People who say an opportunity can be created are the ones who are successful and possess foresight.

Rightly so, men and women are opposite sexes – they have been opposing one another since the beginning of history.

Keeping oneself busy may not be as virtuous as one thinks; it all depends on what one is doing.

You may be ignorant. But to be ignorant of your

ignorance is unforgivable.

Man is such a funny creature; he always believes he is knowledgeable even though he is ignorant.

Ignorance is not as blissful as you might want to think. In fact it can be very painful.

Self-deception is the worst illusion of all illusions.

Imagination works wonders; it provides the poor with the only hope to go on living.

For many, imagination is not very different from day-dreaming; for a few, it is the source of great ideas.

To imitate others to improve yourself is fine, but to keep on imitating your old self is simply pathetic.

Again, if you continue playing with imitation, you are putting a limit on your own ability.

When you say, 'I'm moral,' you are fairly near to *immoral* with only the apostrophe dropped.

When you say, 'I'm mortal,' surely you are not claiming to be immortal.

So, like many others, you crave for immortality. Since you are not getting it in this life, you look for a life after, and after, and after.

Only those dead people whose words and deeds are still alive have attained immortality.

In many instances, it takes time to do the difficult things, and it takes just a little bit more time to do the seemingly impossible ones.

There are many impossible things, but there are many more impossible people.

Do not be misled by people who use a lot of impressive words; chances are the words are hollow and may not mean anything at all.

Never feel depressed because you are unable to impress; chances are you may have suppressed yourself.

Fiction may be scary, truth can be worse.

We live in a flux of change. There is nothing wrong with change except when it changes for the worse.

How many men are victims of their own impulses? One pays a very dear price for indulging in impulses.

How could you know you are unable to do something without giving it a try?

As a lifelong teacher, I would want to see more children searching for knowledge rather than knowledge looking for children.

I would also want to see more good teachers. Imagine the harm that has been done to children by weak teachers.

For many students, especially the less able ones, it is better to have no teachers than bad teachers.

We have made a very big mistake. We tend to think that any Tom, Dick or Harry can be a teacher. So we pay teachers little, and for that we are paying a very heavy price.

We have two ears, two eyes and a mouth. It implies that we need to listen and observe at least twice as much as we talk.

If someone does not speak well it does not mean he does not know well. His thoughts run too fast for his speech to catch up.

A person who speaks well is not necessarily knowledgeable. He may be skilful at repeating his idea using different phrases and sentences.

We always talk behind others – the safest way of avoiding being beaten up.

Some people may not be as smart as you think, they are just being tactfully smart.

To be tactful is to know when far is too far.

Tact is a special technique involving applying the right cosmetics at the right time.

A tactful person is one who knows how to make you feel good when insulted.

How many people get to be happy out of sympathy for others who are in trouble?

Genuine sympathy is hard to come by. Treasure it when it drops by.

Some Japanese are said to ease their stress by smashing china plates. An easier way is to swear them away when taking showers.

Swearing may be psychologically sound; however, do it when no one else is around.

We tend to think that women are more prone to suspicion than men; in fact, some men are much worse.

When one gets suspicious in everything, one's life is simply pathetic and miserable.

We are often suspicious of others, so why can't we be suspicious of our own intentions?

If you do not want others to be suspicious of you, you must not suspect them in the first place.

Life is full of surprises, the good as well as the bad ones. Things happen when you least expect them.

It's not that there are insufficient resources for the world's population; the problem is one of unequal distribution and incomparable consumption.

Faith and superstition are hard to differentiate; it depends on who the person is. One person's faith can well be another person's superstition.

Taking other people's possessions is a crime, taking your own is not (except attempting to take your own life). Since when has suicide become a philosophical problem?

If this life is full of suffering, how can one be so sure that the next one is not?

The person who gives in when wrong is smart; the person who gives in when right is sagacious.

Education helps one to build up knowledge and character, but it does not make a fool wise.

The wonderful thing about education is that the more you study the less you think you know.

Study depresses me. The more I study, the more I believe I am ignorant.

There is only one thing more stretchable than a spring – a lie. A spring may reach its elastic limit, a lie never.

It is completely crazy: you work hard to save for your old age, only to discover that you are not in the position to enjoy the fruits of your labour.

Statues are for the maniacs. Truly great men do not need any monument.

Statistics have become really powerful. They can show you everything you have wanted to show.

The members of a committee have finally come to terms: they have agreed to be disagreeable, and decided to be indecisive.

Each person tends to have three faces at any given time: one he wants others to see, one as others see him, and the third his real face.

Never indulge in your impulses, lest you regret too late.

Many a man is lazy not because he wants to be, but because his body provides too much inertia for him to overcome.

Remember, spare the cane, spoil the kid, regret the parents.

No one can make a person feel small unless that

person submits.

Education is in jeopardy. The paradox is that many of those who want to study cannot study because they are poor, and others who can afford to study do not want to study.

If infidelity was a punishable crime, the world would need ten times more prisons.

Do not judge a married man by his behaviour. If he is good, it's probable he may not be *that* good.

Inflation is a norm, and unidirectional. Things get more expensive at the very time when money gets smaller – never the other way round.

Women make men philosophers, men make women talkers.

Nowadays, it seems futile to influence your children in any way – they always seem to know a better way.

Information is not knowledge. Downloading information from computers does not necessary constitute learning.

Man redefined: a two-legged, ungrateful, selfish, insatiable, and sick mammal.

Information can mean different things to different people: those who want to use it, those who want to keep it and those who want to tell it to others.

Choice of Words

How can a government which is consistently and persistently robbing Peter to give to Paul survive for such long time? Can nothing really be done about it? Nothing. This is because Peter belongs to a minority group and Paul holds the majority votes.

It is not the weight of a woman that counts, it is where she carries it that matters.

Few men can restrain themselves at the sight of a lady's teardrops.

On the other hand, women should not use their sobs to subdue their men.

If you have the possibility of a divorce at the back of your mind right at the very beginning, don't jump into your wedding gown at all.

There are two things that are more easily said than done: an empty promise and the marriage oath.

Meteorologists are people with guts. They dare to predict the unpredictable.

To a large extent, the atmospheric pressure dictates man's pleasure: a high atmospheric pressure brings pleasure, a low one otherwise.

The car was invented to compensate for the advance in medical science. As fewer and fewer people die of disease, more and more people are killed on the roads.

Isn't it ironic? On the one hand, the army is furiously attacking the enemy, while on the other hand, the medical team is busily carrying the wounded or dead soldiers away.

Ignorance can be blissful when your spouse is having an extramarital affair and when your income tax department forgets to bill you.

Not many people would be able to claim that they are on the way to success and fame, for the great majority of them will be still on their way till their very last day.

Water can be most deceptive: a swimming pool always appears much shallower, and a ruler appears to bend in it.

Watches nowadays come in all types of proofs: waterproof, shockproof, pressure-proof – but not thief-proof.

One-third of the world's population use paper every day. If one person uses one piece of paper less, then you can save two billion pieces of paper per day. Do you know how much energy and how many trees may be saved in this way?

Our computers are supposed to save paper. How is it that more and more paper is used to download more and more stuff from the Internet and print emails?

Beware, do not jump to conclusions, because you are likely to land up with concussions.

Basically, man is a rather conceited creature: our

success is due to our effort, our failure is due to bad fortune.

Swollen heads are like empty vessels – they sound hollow.

A conceited person is one who wears an oversized magnifying glass when looking at his own achievements – everything is blown up out of proportion.

Computers are truly gentlemen, they never blame anybody for mistakes made by anyone (including the programmers).

Computers have been, and still are, superb unpaid servants. Just wait till the day when they turn into calculating paymasters!

Many conferences and seminars (be they local, regional or international) provide great opportunities for big talkers. They have since relegated to more of a social gathering than the meeting of thinkers and the pooling of ideas. The main output is often the decision about the when and where of the next conference or seminar.

Nobody seems to want to take the trouble to have a follow-up assessment to find out if the objectives of a conference are being achieved. Why have the conference in the first place?

Pretend to confide in your friend, and observe how he or she is taken in even by your most extravagant lie.

There are quite a few probabilities involved in a

medical doctor's diagnosis, especially so when the disease is a rare one. Thus, do not get unduly worried when you have an exactly opposite second opinion.

There is no such thing as confusing facts. Facts are facts and cannot be confused. The confusion can only come from confusing reports or hearsay.

If you think you are confused because of the many facts available, see that you are not more confused in the absence of facts.

People without conscience can be happy. But the happiest people are those with a clear conscience.

For many people, their conscience comes to visit once in a while, especially just before they want to go to sleep.

Not all conscientious people have a conscience, but all people with a conscience are conscientious.

A considerate person can tolerate a situation only to a certain extent, whereas a tolerant person will tolerate the most inconsiderate situation.

Every one has the right to consume – but of course only when they have the money.

It may be fine to consume the reproducible stuff, but it is unforgivable to consume relentlessly the non-renewable resources. Our descendants are going to pay a very high price for our follies.

When you are faced with a much stronger opponent, the best way of beating him is to walk away in silent contempt.

Can the poor be contented? Some rich people think they are. This must be the worst misconception which persists in the minds of the rich.

When we say a contented man is not poor, we do not necessarily mean that he is literally not a poor man.

One small secret of being contented: if you do not have what you'd love to have, love what you already have.

Numerous contracts and agreements are signed every day, everywhere. The only conclusion one can draw from such rampancy of mutual understandings is that man has become less and less trustworthy, so much so that word of mouth is of no use or consequence any more.

Come to think of it, if everyone is honest and can be trusted under all circumstances, what are rules and regulations for? There would not be any need to have law enforcers or lawyers anymore.

How About That?

If a two-dimensional picture is worth a thousand words, a three-dimensional model will be worth ten thousand words; for the simple reason that the latter can be viewed in a variety of perspectives and from many different angles.

Even a three-dimensional model cannot match the real experience in the right setting. Often the true experience is beyond any description.

When is a misconception a misconception? It is when you obstinately refuse to change your wrong concept despite the evidence which shows otherwise.

A century ago, workers were called to unite to bring down capitalism. A decade ago, workers called themselves to unite to bring down communism. The twenty-first century will witness workers uniting to bring down computer-ism.

Today is 2.2.2000, a date with all even digits made up of 2s and 0s. The last such even digit date was 28.8.888, 1111 years ago. The last all-odd-digit date was 19.11.1999, made up of 1s and 9s, and the next such date will be 1.1.3111, 1111 years later.

1998 was a wonderful year. The digits of 1998 add up to 27, a multiple of 3.

Divide 1998 by 2, you get 999 which is divisible by 3,

and its digits add up to 27.

Divide 1998 by 3, you get 666 which is divisible by 3, and its digits add up to 18.

Divide 1998 by 6, you get 333 which is divisible by 3, and its digits add up to 9.

Divide 1998 by 9, you get 222 which is divisible by 3, and its digits add up to 6.

Divide 1998 by 18, you get 111 which is still divisible by 3, its digits add up to 3.

All the numbers 27, 18, 9, 6, 3 are multiples of 3.

The shortest distance between poverty and wealth is a deceptively crooked and jagged line. The shortest distance between destitution and fame is a surprisingly straight line with many kinks and snaps in between.

Make hay while the sun shines, but do not make wine while the moon shines.

Two wrongs certainly cannot make one right, neither do two left turns make one right turn.

Life is but a probability, right from the time of conceiving. It is a probability of the most ingenious and unsolvable kind.

Life is an arduous but inescapable journey. Some of us have long and fruitful journeys, others' are unbelievably short and insignificant. Some journeys are smooth and straight, others bumpy and battered, yet others windy and wretched.

Flowers are not just meant to be looked at. Their fragrance is meant to be smelled and their texture felt.

A person may be blunt, but he is the sharpest in front

of his opponents.

You are a greater fool if you cannot recognise the fools around you.

It takes a fool to tell you that he is not a fool while others are.

Praise a person, and you see how fast you get the returns.

Old age is a bane. Can you imagine an elderly person behaving like a foolish boy?

Not all food can be bought and eaten. Try, for instance, food for thought.

The question of nature versus nurture may soon be settled. Genetic engineering will soon make nurture redundant.

I am completely dumbfounded by so many things that can be made 'instant' nowadays. We have instant food, instant drinks, an instant diploma, instant parents and worst of all instant gratification of all kinds.

In this world of competition (or is it collaboration?), things are moving fast and life is hectic. Wise is the person who knows how to keep calm under all circumstances.

Don't just look before you leap; you should think (at least twice) before you act. Indeed, you would be just another lame duck if you think and don't act.

If you do not want to mind your own business, wait till you see what happens when *other* people begin to mind your business for you.

It is not uncommon for innocent old ladies to be cheated by con men of their hard-earned life savings. How people can do such despicable thing is beyond my understanding.

Computers are getting more and more powerful at a frightening speed. The awesome impact they have on ordinary people is beyond description. Nevertheless, do not be misled into assuming that a computer is fault-proof and does not make mistakes. If so, then unfortunately that will be man's gravest mistake.

If you are so busy that you have no time to think about whether you are busy or not, then you are the happiest man on earth.

Bureaucracy is a self-contained system. It is invented by the group of people for their own benefit at the expense of the public.

Why do you need a budget when you have no money to spend?

The person who knows how to budget well is the one who understands economy.

There is always a bright side to everything, except that the other side is dark.

A baby will brighten your days, yet equally often darken your nights.

Power corrupts, absolute power corrupts absolutely. Super-power intoxicates, absolute super-power intoxicates absolutely. Is this happening to the USA now?

The word 'live' when spelt backwards becomes 'evil'. To live is to face evil, evil of different degrees and magnitudes.

The only other four-letter word that can be formed from the letters of 'love' is 'vole'. Vole means a rodent. Is love the rodent in disguise?

If you cannot flatter a woman about her beauty, the least you can do is to tell her how intelligent she is.

The best way to flatter a person is to let him know that he is a person who does not like to be flattered.

Talk can be empty and futile, but not if you have enough flowers to be distributed.

There's a big question of unequal distribution. The rich have so much food left over after each banquet that it is enough to feed a poor family for an entire month.

The rich have so much food that they have long lost their appetite. The poor have so little food that their appetite has long stopped functioning.

A simpleton's foolishness can be ignored, but a wise man's foolishness leaves one flabbergasted.

In retrospect, many people have wonderful hindsight. However, it is not the hindsight that makes the world what it is, it is the foresight that moves the world.

How often do you forget the person who owes you a favour?

An accurate foresight is worth more than a thousand hindsights.

Forgive your enemies, that is a sure way of making them miserable.

Nothing is absolutely free, not even the clean air you are breathing; you pay a price (albeit a small one, and in different kinds) for everything.

There is no such thing as complete freedom of speech in a democratic society, let alone in an autocratic environment. It is not freedom in the true sense of the word. There is always a hidden censor somewhere along the line.

Keep Talking

'Statistics lie' – so goes a popular aphorism. Actually, good statistics with an accurate supporting explanation provide a useful and precise summary. Statistics only lie in the hands of the uninitiated and those who have vested interest.

Want to know the power of statistics? Try stock market indices.

How many smart people lead a common life simply because they do not make enough effort to overcome their intellectual timidity?

Never take anything at face value or any conclusion for granted. Learn to question the hidden assumptions and rationale.

Think before you speak, more so when you know little about the subject you wish to talk about. Indeed, in such circumstances, it is better to listen.

Familiarity breeds contempt. Why should this be applicable to married life?

You are confronted and clouded with information, data, statistics and facts at every moment. Can you distinguish their differences?

Say what you mean, and mean what you say. How many of us can actually achieve this?

Do not allow familiarity to blur your objectivity, or else you will regret it soon.

If animals were to build a zoo, where and how do you think they would keep man?

A chimpanzee stares hard at the zoo keeper and wonders: Am I keeping my common ancestor brother inside the fence, or is he keeping me inside it?

Why not let old age take its course gracefully, instead of humiliating yourself by keeping disgracefully young?

The present younger generation thinks they know far better than their elders. Just wait for another twenty-five years.

At 6, you do not know what living is; at 16, you think you will live long; and when you reach 60, you may be asking how you have lived that long.

For most senior citizens, it would be fine to think they are still young, except that they do not go out of their way to prove it.

When we were young, we hardly seemed to know that we were young. Now that we are old, we keep thinking we are old.

Today is a very short bridge between yesterday and tomorrow, but this is the very bridge we must cross safely and with dignity.

If you have done nothing wrong yesterday, and keep yourself virtuous today, then what is there to be afraid about tomorrow?

You think you are somebody when you try to please everybody. You end up with nobody.

Many a woman of sixty years old would have spent twenty years in sleeping, three years in eating and drinking, ten years in personal chores, make-up and dressing, and the rest of the time in either working, bringing up the family, nagging or gossiping.

I have been both pessimistic and negative in my remarks in many instances. I believe this is largely due to my past experience. Is it not true that people are often shaped by their past?

In theory, politics should be divorced from education; in practice politics is married to education. Practice wins.

Those who think, write; those who talk, do not write.

If you cannot write, be an editor; or better still, a critic.

There is a trick in writing: either put old wine in a new bottle or put new wine in an old bottle. In fact both methods work.

Authors enjoy a very special position. They can put down words you dislike but need not be afraid of being confronted by you.

Time is a marvellous ruler for line drawing, it draws lines on everybody's face.

Before you press the car accelerator down hard, just recall for a moment the wreckage in the junkyard.

If a book you are reading is not measuring up to your expectation, do not blame the author, condemn the publisher.

If you accept everything a book says, you may as well not read it, even it is a book about science.

A best-seller is not necessarily a good book, it is the seller at his best.

A really good book is like a huge flat mirror, it reflects your true self. Most books, unfortunately, are like curved mirrors: the convex ones make you look smaller, and the concave ones either make you look larger or upside down.

When two bores talk to each other, they are wide awake, making sure the other will not fall asleep.

Why are only the bores allowed to have so much free time – usually someone else's free time?

A sure way of losing a friendship is to borrow money from your friend.

A learned man is not necessarily measured by the number of books nicely stacked along his shelves. He may be a learned decorator, though.

A good book is meant to be read and digested, not just displayed.

A lady is attractive despite her cosmetics; a book is useful despite its cover.

Marriage is a tussle between husband and wife, mainly about who should be the boss.

When the boss laughs, every one laughs – albeit superficially; when he cries, he cries alone.

This is one's life history: bossed by mother, then by sister(s), followed by wife, and daughter(s) – in that chronological order.

A child is always a child, a boy a boy, a man a man, an old man an old man; but not a very old man, because he is a child.

Someone can be brainy, but he may not be an intellectual.

The mass of an average man is probably slightly greater than that of an average woman (whatever the word 'average' may mean). This is because man needs that extra bit to understand woman, and perhaps outwit her at times.

Keeps on Oozing Out of my Head

Education has fast become a hot commodity in the last two decades, traded between the knows and know-nots. Just look at the mushrooming of tertiary institutions whose intentions have more to do with business than education, selling cheap diplomas to the uninitiated.

After more than thirty-four years of teaching, I have come to a sad conclusion. We have many seemingly knowledgeable people (albeit more often than not half-baked and semi-literate), yet we do not find one-quarter as many educated people.

Since when did professors sell their knowledge, politicians their promises, salespersons their mouths, lawyers their conscience and doctors their practice?

I do not mind people. It is their pretence and vanity that I cannot stand.

Trying to make new year resolutions again? Better not, chances are they will still be like pre-dated blank cheques – not honoured by any bank.

The weakest point about science is that it cannot grapple with irrationality, in particular, the inexplicable irrational behaviour of women.

If you are talented, it is not necessary that you are a genius. If you are a genius, it is not necessary that you are normal; you can be either abnormal or subnormal. Which is which?

It's not that men are faithless, it is just that they cannot resist the multitudes of temptations not of their making. They are their own unfortunate victims.

How often does one's fantasy run wild before sleep? One thinks of the impossible, one hopes for the impossible and then one falls asleep to make the impossible possible in one's dreams.

Women are generous. They are generous when you shower them with praise and flattery. But the generosity turns ugly as soon as you unintentionally prick their pride.

You just cannot be too careful in life. You may have done a thousand good things and, not being appreciated, a small mistake disproportionately exaggerated will land you in hot soup in no time.

It is not that I am antisocial, but somehow I feel that it is a criminal waste of time in indulging in unnecessary tale-telling and unfounded gossiping, all of which benefit no one in the least.

Forty years ago, a young man would say to his parents, 'You have brought me up well, now is my turn to look after you at your old age.' Nowadays, a young person may tell his parents, 'It was your duty to feed me and educate me, now you should be able to look after yourselves at old age.'

How many an elderly wife would prefer to take care of her daughter's children rather than to stay with her old spouse? There are many examples among my contemporaries.

If liberal education is so liberal that one doesn't need to sweat to obtain a degree or diploma, what then is the worth of a liberal paper qualification?

Clean air is still free for most people on earth, but clean water comes with a small price in many countries. There will be a day when pollution is uncontrollable and there are so many people fighting for clean air and clean water; then both will become scarce and come with expensive price tags.

Why should there be freedom of speech when the speeches made in free time are practically free of substance?

There may be freedom of speech. However, the speech itself may not be free. It may cost you a fortune if someone finds fault and makes a scandal out of it.

Freedom of speech does not necessarily mean that speeches are free. It is definitely not cheap talk, which is next to nonsense.

Your good friend may stab you from behind whereas your enemy may prefer a frontal attack.

Often old friends seem to be better friends, after all their trustworthiness has already been tested for that many years.

What is a true friend? The one who will see you through thick and thin while others have already seen that you were through.

You cannot have the cake and eat it. Likewise, you cannot have a friend and use him.

Many a young person does not quite believe that one cannot have the cake and eat it. He thinks that there is nothing wrong in having the cake and eating it at the same time.

If you know how to appreciate a good friend, then you will have no difficulty in shovelling away an enemy.

It may be true that money cannot buy you love, but it does make it easy for you to find those who are ready to sell you love.

It may also be true that money cannot buy you true friends, but it certainly helps your enemies to sell you.

In all circumstances and situations, do not talk without thinking about what you want to say first. An impromptu and hasty remark may make you spend more time thinking about it later.

Someone said friendship is like a bank account, one cannot keep drawing from it without depositing. I said friendship cannot be like a bank account: you can walk away with a loan from a bank within minutes – but try this on a friend.

What makes you think that having fun is life? Do you not see that fun disguises itself as fund and funk?

We old people surely cannot be so naïve as to think that the modern youth will have the same value system as we had in our younger days. If we do, we are asking for trouble, the magnitude of which may be beyond our imagination, and so be prepared to face the unexpected.

Someone said that a lady's voice is so sweet as to make the birds stop chirping to listen to her. How could this be true when birds are seemingly oblivious to the human voice? Perhaps this is where the strength of a beautiful metaphor lies.

Old age is the bane of one's life. Even insurance companies charge a premium in direct proportion to your age.

Have you ever been confronted by your child asking you, 'See what you have done to me? I did not ask to be born to face all these miseries of life in the first place!'? What will your answer be?

You may want to think that all men were born equal. However, the truth is that some were born more equal than many others.

In marriage, the better half will turn the bitter half sooner than most of us would ever dare to think.

It is far too easy to tell a lie. The difficult part is how to invent ten more lies just to cover the first lie.

White lies are supposed to be harmless lies. Nonetheless, if they are handled and passed too often, especially by dirty hands, then they become dirty lies.

Money does not really always talk, more so if it is the silent cash stacked in an offshore bank.

Silence in a court of law is not necessarily that golden, unless of course you are already prepared to stay behind iron bars.

You are quick in blaming others for your misfortune. People call this human nature. The same human nature will be even quicker to congratulate you when fortune descends. How strange!

Do not assume that by saying nothing, doing nothing and pretending to be nothing, you can get away from being blamed. Blame is like a faithful shadow, tracing every step you take, unless of course you stay in the dark all the time. Even that itself is likely to bring you a bit of blame.

Is That So?

He whose laugh lasted, laughed best. He whose thought lasted, thought best.

Always keep an open mind, no matter how bizarre the information appears.

All of us have brains, but do we all have minds?

Where is the dichotomy of mind and matter, if mind is taken to mean the grey matter?

By nature man is already pathetic, yet man makes himself more pathetic by his human nature.

Show me a person who has not made any mistake in life, and I shall show you another with three eyes.

Man is attracted to money like bees to honey. They can never have enough.

Like most value systems, morality is relativistic. Someone said morality is feeling good after doing something, and immorality is not feeling good.

Hunger and morality have been at loggerheads since time immemorial. Staying alive takes the priority.

Scandals are multiplicative, especially when loads of dirt are added on each time – soon a molehill will turn into a mountain.

The most beautiful part of a musical performance is

the dead silence just before the applause.

If you do not like any music, you probably do not like anything at all in life.

I am poor at remembering names; I may forget mine too one day. After all, what is in a name?

Romance is child's play. He who believes in romance is probably just fantasising.

Never let vengeance engulf you. When vengeance strikes, it strikes hard and cruel – including your own self.

People holding jobs retire when the time comes. Have you heard of housewives and writers retiring?

The world will be a much more peaceful place if each and every one of us knows our duties and responsibilities well.

You can lose your money, you can lose your career, but never lose your self-respect.

Why repent when your conscience is clear?

I am certainly growing older; my reminiscence is fast catching up with me, though my memory keeps failing me.

All religions are inevitably good, but a person should be given that little freedom to find the path to heaven in his own way.

One can find one's own god in any religion, as long as there is faith.

Mathematical formulae are useless in human

relationships, more so in religion.

Man claims to be the supreme animal because he can reason. By any measure, man is good at reasoning, except he is just not that reasonable.

A man is better judged by the questions he asked, and not the answers he gave.

As long as it is not true, why would I care what people say about me?

Before the profession of psychiatry existed, no parents had been blamed for their children misdeeds.

What is the difference between a whore and a promiscuous woman? One takes money, the other declines.

Save a dollar for a rainy day, save another in case it does not.

Time has changed. In this modern era, almost all of us are a bit neurotic as a result of struggling to keep our noses above troubled waters.

Past, present, and future is a continuum – one cannot exist without the others.

Nowadays, it is hard to find a patient person – everybody seems to be hurriedly going nowhere, or maybe somewhere.

Do not aim for perfection; it never exists, it has never meant to be.

Once bitten, twice shy. Never – persevere and move on!

Man is a pest to mankind; unfortunately, he has not become aware of it.

People want to be praised, but who would want to be appraised?

The world is swarming with questions beginning with What, Why, Who, Where, When and How. Precisely, I shall be asking more and more questions of this nature.

Let there be more peace on earth…

More About That

When the computer becomes more complicated and complex, its complexity may turn into complicity. Such complex complicity will not help the lesser initiated users and make the computer less user-friendly.

When the computer gets too smart, it may not be a healthy sign for the public. By and large it could do more harm than good.

Advanced technology will be useful for mankind if there is a guarantee that it will not be manipulated by unscrupulous people and that it is programmed in such a way that the ultimate command still lies in the hands of man. If there is no such guarantee, we may be courting a catastrophe of which we have only the faintest idea.

After microchips, next comes nano-chips. When nano-chips get into man's brain, it is the beginning of the end of mankind – there will only be robot-kind.

The world is moving towards a button-pressing globe. There is nothing wrong with this button-pressing world if only people know when and where to press the right buttons.

The Chinese call a computer an 'electronic brain'. As it is, the computer is not that brainy, as yet. But then, who knows, one day it may outperform the brain. That will be the time when man should seriously reassess his role in this world.

A fool is soon parted from his money. How is it that nobody asks where the money came from in the first place? Moreover, can a fool really make that much money?

If your employer wants you for the job, he can give one thousand reasons to keep you. On the other hand if he does not need you anymore, he needs to invent only one reason to sack you.

A little flattery will help a man to quench his thirst; unfortunately, too much of it will drown him in no time.

See the way how a politician who stands for election shakes people's hands before voting day. Notice how he sits in a chauffeured car after being elected.

People want to have a share of the money in a capitalistic country, but people are forced to share miseries in a communist country.

I wonder what would Karl Marx say if he were still alive. Would he say, 'How bitter can it be when one is forced to eat one's own words.'?

Communism would have been fine if only man were less capitalism-oriented.

Do not be misguided by the argument that modern technology has enabled cars to be made fast yet safe. Physics reveals that a fast car is always a dangerous car.

Never in the history of mankind have there been so many people riding in motor vehicles; likewise, never in the history of mankind have so many people been destroyed by motor vehicles.

What an irony! It is now much quicker to cover a 1,000 km journey by plane to the next city than to drive the 30 km from the city to the airport.

One would think that car is a convenient and fast means of transportation. Not so anymore; an average city car at peak period moves hardly more than 10 km per hour – far slower than a marathon runner.

It was reported that thirty people were killed and several hundred injured in the first day of the Chinese New Year (5.2.2000) in Malaysia. What a terrible man-made carnage! How could such destruction of human lives be allowed to go on by man's own invention?

Life is a gamble which takes many forms. One thing is for sure, never lay down your trump card too soon, or you will have nothing else worth revealing.

One cannot be too careful in choosing one's lifetime partner. A slight slip will be sufficient to land oneself in quicksand.

Credit cards are wonderful things. They prevent you from paying through the nose by making you put down a signature.

Another smart thing a smart card does is to blur your mind into thinking, 'Have card, will travel'. All transactions are made easy and painless, especially when you don't have to carry as well as count bundles of notes.

Don't you think we are all subtly conned by our cards and psychologically controlled by them?

It is certainly not wise to let your cat out of the bag too soon. The cat will be out of sight before you realise you have made a mistake.

Behind a successful man there's always a capable woman – a woman capable of making you hunt for money and fame day and night.

Can you be more cautious than the person who always looks right, left and then right again while crossing a one-way street?

Many of us are coy enough to say that we dislike flattery, yet deep inside us we are waiting anxiously for it.

Be careful, don't start doing something else when you are still in the process of doing another thing – always do one thing at a time, and one thing after another.

A celebrity is someone who only smiles in front of a public video or camera. The smile is more a pretence than anything else.

You cannot be so naïve as to think that a celebrity knows you when she is smiling at you. No, she has forced herself into a smile in order to create the right image of a celebrity.

Censorship does not often make sense. A censor has lots of senses, except common sense – the sense common people possess.

If you have nothing else better to do, be a censor and be sensible.

Conviction is the prelude to success. Not necessarily so, unless the conviction is of the right kind.

Nothing is certain in life, except death – its probability is exactly 1.

Nothing is permanent in this world. Everything changes with time, including man, except man changes more often and in a much shorter time.

We all have several characters – one in public, one in the workplace, one in the company of close friends, one in the family and one when alone. Our true character is the one when we are alone.

Old Sayings – New Interpretations

★ *Honesty is the best policy* – You are stupid to be honest. The more dishonest you are, the smarter and better you become; surely you will be rich and powerful sooner.

★ *Penny wise, pound foolish* – You do not go for the penny nowadays, you hit straight at the pound. The faster you do this, the quicker you will accumulate your wealth.

★ *Killing two birds with one stone* – You certainly want to eliminate more than two birds without any stone, or best without any effort at all. Look for shortcuts and loop holes, be thick-skinned and do not blush.

★ *Beggars do not bargain* – Watch out for cunning beggars in disguise. Not only will they bargain hard, they will try to strip you naked or even wipe you out.

★ *Once bitten, twice shy* – This does not apply to modern man. When it comes to personal advantage and benefit, you won't want to shy away after being bitten. You will persevere and hit back and get what you are looking for.

★ *Look before you leap* – How many of you would want to look first before you undertake anything? You plunge straight into it, ignoring whatever consequence that may arise, good or bad. Would you want to listen to anybody?

★ *Turn over a new leaf* – You may ask, Why turn over the leaf when both sides of it are similar   in   nature   or colour? Who would not want to enjoy life as long as they can, instead of forfeiting their ill-gotten fortune?

★ *Rolling stones gather no moss* – Things are very different today. The more you know how to roll, the more income you get, the more power you possess and the more famous you become.

★ *A stitch in time saves nine* – Things are not made to last, right? They are meant to be replaced by new ones, the sooner the better. This is how economy grows. When it is time for making a stitch, it is time to replace.

★ *Beauty is skin deep* – No, not any more. Cosmetic surgery goes beyond the skin. It penetrates deep into the flesh to be filled up by silicate jelly and whatnot at a steep price. However, you do not often get what you want.

★ *Rome was not built in a day* – To the new generation, time is money. Everything is associated with instant-aneous accomplishment. If you can build Rome within one hour, why not? Get it done at super-speed, then you will be super-rich instantly.

★ *Money cannot buy everything* – No, no, you are obsolete. Money is the demigod, all-permeating, all-powerful. It is the modern genie of the magic lamp. Just command the genie, it will do practically everything for you: love, women, men, anything… After all, tell me what is not for sale today?

★ *You must love your neighbours* – In city-life, do you

really know your neighbours? Most buildings (naturally, the worst are the tall flats and apartments) are constructed and fenced to isolate occupants in their respective cubicles. So, if you do not even know your neighbours, can you love them? Yes, if you are that compassionate, why not?

⋆ *Time and tide wait for no man* – Are you sure? If you can be cloned, you are going to be ageless, as ageless as the tide and time. It will come to a time when you will be waiting for the time and tide, not the other way round.

⋆ *A bird in the hand is worth two in the bush* – This cannot be true any more, especially if the bird in hand is a dead or useless bird. For many people, one bird in the hand is definitely not enough. They want more, many more, alive and beautiful ones. Once their hands are full, they will use cages to trap those in the bushes. Why not?

⋆ *Do not count the chickens before they are hatched* – You are certainly not catching up with the modern wonders of science and medicine. Medical scientists are able to determine even the sex of the fertilised egg, and whether the baby to be born is suffering from any physiological defects or undesirable anomalies – a lot more than just simple counting.

⋆ *Do not teach your grandmother how to suck eggs* – Again, you are behind the times. 'Life-long learning' is the latest catchphrase. Whether you like it or not, you have to learn and learn throughout your life. Things are changing so fast nowadays that you have no choice but to relearn old stuff in a new perspective, and the new ideas perhaps from an old perspective. Grandmothers must be taught to handle new gadgets they would never have dreamt of.

* *Curiosity killed the cat* – You are dead wrong! Children are by nature curious. When students learn science in schools, they are told to be curious and be sufficiently motivated by their curiosity. Cats have nine lives – that is what people used to say (never mind if it is true or not). Not only will curiosity not kill the cat, it won't kill us either.

* *God helps those who help themselves* – This is probably the only statement still true to some extent, that is, if God is there. Who would not want to help himself first? How many of us are that selfless as to help every other person beside ourselves? You will be lucky if someone is not out to slight you or demean you. Help yourself first, right? (I had better stop mentioning God, lest I will be accused of blasphemy or insolence.)

Some Observations

If seeing a black cat running across the street on Friday the 13th is not taken as bad luck by a mouse, why should it be bad luck for man?

How is it that some superstitious beliefs continue to pervade human minds? Can there be an acceptable explanation?

Why, deep down our hearts, so many of us cannot wait to see other people unhappy?

We all want to be happy. In the pursuit of happiness, how many of us have often inadvertently stepped onto the path of unhappiness?

Come to think of it, a little unhappiness, some discontentment, and a bit of anxiety will make life more challenging and sustainable.

Do you feel moody just because you suspect that many people are happier than you?

The amount of umbrella cover a man gives to a woman during a rainy day is a good indicator of their relationship.

So you really want to know the truth? It all depends on your ability in filtering away all the lies that have clouded the truth.

You do not need any other truth to support a truth;

however, you need at least ten lies to cover a lie.

Lies are sweeter than truth, only the fools do not seem to know that.

Truths are often ugly, perhaps that is why people seeking for beauty avoid them most of the time.

To trust everyone is one thousand times worse than not trusting anyone. On the other hand, life would be miserable if you have no one to trust.

Your enemies are of your own making. Chances are that you're the one who creates them.

If other people make you their enemy, why worry? They are the ones who will suffer, worrying about why you are their enemy.

The best way to treat a person who thinks you are his foe is to befriend him – this will drive him nuts.

All animals need loving care. Do you not know that patting a horse is more effective than kicking its back?

Encouragement is free on your part, but it becomes very valuable to the person you have just encouraged.

How can employers expect young graduates in their early twenties to have had five years of experience? Experience in what?

Too many young tertiary education graduates are looking for positions nowadays; they don't actually take the job, nor do they really want the work.

Here is a something beyond one's understanding: a person stealing a $10 object is likely to land himself in jail, whereas another person squandering $10,000,000 is most probably enjoying himself in another country.

If you think electricity is not cheap, try living for a day or two without electricity.

Don't be too harsh on an egotist, at least he knows many things about himself other people don't.

His trouble is not that he has no character, he has too many – a different one each day.

Why are so many of us inclined to be dissatisfied with things around us? And more so, when we have things we do not deserve.

Someone who has to hide his true emotions in public every day, will have little choice but to explode with the pent-up emotion at the slightest provocation at home once in a while, like a firework display.

Putting a person to a vote of confidence is a subtle way of telling him that people simply have no confidence in him.

If you marry a highly suspicious and constantly nagging wife, you may as well be half-deaf, semi-blind and ready to confine yourself within four walls.

If you marry a tempestuous and elusive husband, be prepared to toughen up your spirit and mental strength – of course, another option would be a divorce.

Better get married to a caring though plain-looking woman rather than one who is pretty but vain.

What is the use of having a solemn lifelong partnership promise during your wedding when the door to eventual divorce is already wide open?

Lack of understanding produces a marriage; complete understanding underlines the cause of divorce.

When opportunity comes, it knocks only once; when misfortune visits, it comes in bundles and breaks down the door.

The things I treasure most in life are my dreams – they make impossible things possible.

The things I dislike most in life are my nightmares – they make possible things impossible.

It's a vicious cycle: drinking brings people mishaps, and mishaps lead to more drinking.

Does drinking really drown one's sorrows? Hardly; it just helps to put aside the sorrow temporarily.

Once the sorrow resurfaces, one needs more drinks to push it away. So it goes on until one gets drunk, only to be confronted by the sorrow the following day again.

I do not mind people driving a bit fast if they drive with care, but I detest those who drive recklessly, oblivious to the safety of other road users.

It is hard to be careful when one drives very fast; a slight error will likely to cause an accident – killing not only the driver but also endangering the lives of other drivers and passengers.

Rash overtaking is one of the main factors of accidents on country roads, it has claimed far more precious lives than one can imagine.

If you drive like hell, you will reach there much sooner than you think.

Most women have three important duties to carry out in life: the first is making themselves beautiful, the second is keeping themselves pretty, and the third is sustaining their attractiveness.

We can shut our eyes with ease, we can close our mouths without much difficulty, but it is almost impossible to block our ears completely. Why?

I wonder if we are all lunatics living in a huge asylum called earth.

To eat to live is humane; can living to eat be more humane?

Before a person's new idea bears fruit, he is crazy. After the new idea materialises, he turns genius overnight.

Economics is a study of how to get rich by spending money.

An economist is one who knows how to borrow $1 and multiply it into $100, and then pocket the $99.

A stock exchange expert will tell you tomorrow why his yesterday's prediction about share prices was not correct today.

The person who stands to gain under all circumstances of market fluctuations is the stockbroker – he gets a commission every time, irrespective of your gain or loss.

Passing Comments

Deception is an art, a really fine art. Some people are so good at it that it becomes their second nature.

Deception is an ancient art. Man has been able to master it so well that it is instrumental in the ticking of our civilisation all these millennia.

If you cheat people of their money, you end up in prison. If you cheat them of their votes, you end up in parliament.

You cannot even deceive a fool all the time, let alone the public.

A deceiver deceives. What do you call a person who deceives the deceiver?

Religion without faith is superficial. Faith without religion is equally superficial.

You can lose all your worldly possessions and still live. How can you lose your faith in life and still live?

Do you still consider women to be the fairer gender? Wait till you meet one of the many iron ladies.

He has not achieved anything in life. It's not that he had no plans, or did not strive for it; it is just that he spent half of his life planning and the other half re-planning.

Though he hardly accomplished anything of significance,

he was certainly not a failure – no one wants to be a failure.

He had lived a simple and peaceful life – that itself was an accomplishment.

Many of us believe that failure is the mother of success, but do not tell this to some one who has not tasted the sweetness of success.

He who cannot capitalise on his failure is doomed to fail again.

If you dare to fail and face it with calmness and dignity, then success is waiting nearby.

Fortune favours and smiles at those who can stand up straight each time after a fall.

Facts loaded with figures can be misleading. Facts without any figures can be even more misleading.

Whenever a person starts using the phrase 'as a matter of fact', what follows will most likely be a matter of non-fact.

A lie repeated a thousand times does not qualify itself to be a fact.

There are so many different and wonderful kinds of masks around that one can hardly tell who is or who isn't wearing one.
In certain cultures, face-saving is of utmost importance. Their motto is, Better die than lose face.

What kind of world will it be if everyone wears the same face (clones aside)?

Genetic engineering has advanced to a frightening and threatening stage. Will those involved ever ask you what type of clone(s) the world requires?

When you have made a decision, do not ponder over it again and again.

Indecision procrastinates, and procrastination is one of the most common human weaknesses.

Do not regret any decision already made, unless it is a rash one; for the decision was probably the best one under the given circumstances at that particular point of time.

If someone is all out to smear you, your best defence is not to defend it – let it wear off by itself.

If someone feels comfortable with his delusions, let him be lest he turns mad.

Democracy is one of the most quoted yet misunderstood word – what a shame.

Democracy is an art, the art of manipulating people. Democracy is a science, the science of people manipulating.

How many governments so far have committed unspeakable crimes and blatant atrocities in the name of democracy?

Under a democratic government, everyone is supposed to have equal rights. Somehow, somewhat, some people are more equal than others.

Why are there so many people willing to offer a remedy for the common cold when there is actually none?

How many people have fallen victims to unconstrained desire and lust? Yet the queue is getting longer and longer.

Diamonds are still a girl's best friend, much to the chagrin of men.

A diamond remains the hardest natural substance known, indeed it is also the hardest substance to get.

If you cannot tell the whole truth, even in your own private diary, you must be a great liar.

Like many other Chinese-educated students, I used to read an English dictionary and remember a number of words by heart – I wonder why I did that, until some of the words surface spontaneously when I need them now.

Someone says that the eyes are the windows of a person's soul – they open up the mind of the person.

How often are a person's inner feelings betrayed by the eyes' expression?

There is still no evidence of extra-terrestrial life. Perhaps there could have been creatures far more advanced than human beings a long time ago on other planets, except for the fact that their super-powerful technology pushed them to extinction much earlier.

A politician is one who is excellent at providing an explanation, except that another person is needed to explain what the explanation is.

It is easy for man to propose now; it will be uneasy for him to be exposed later.

Make sure you can distinguish between an emotional experiment and scientific experiment – one is subjective and the other objective.

Young people nowadays want to learn things the hard way. They would like to experience everything, and perhaps experiment with everything under the sun.

Learning from experience can be painful, but it will be more painful if you do not learn from the experience.

Experiential learning is often costly; for some the experience gained is worth the cost, while for others it would be a sheer waste of money and time.

A smart person always knows when, what, and how to learn from other people's experiences.

Bernard Shaw once remarked that he learned from experience that he never learned from experience. Probably he was unfortunate enough to have only experiences that he did not like.

Experience can be a good teacher, it can also be a bad student.

Experience can be costly, sometimes it costs your life.

Parent: 'Don't do this, you will get hurt. I know this through experience.'
Child: 'Don't deprive me of the chance to gain the experience you once had.'

Prospective employer: 'So you want this job. You have the paper qualification, but you lack experience.'
Eager employee-to-be: 'If you do not take me on, when will I ever have the opportunity to gain experience?'

Do not expect too much from life, for the unexpected often brings you greater joy.

Do not try to show off, you are not far away from a showdown.

Showing off indicates the time when a person has nothing more to show.

This is a world of 'too much'. Some sleep too much, some have too much money, some work too much, some have too much leisure, and the worst is some simply talk too much.

Knowledge tells us the norm, while experience brings us the surprises.

There are things you can stretch, or occasionally over-stretch. The only thing you cannot stretch is truth; once you start stretching truth, it snaps immediately.

Most people tend to exaggerate, some over-exaggerate. Notably, the masters of this latter art are: the journalists, the poets, the newsmakers, the artists, the authors and so on.

If we stick to the theory of evolution, we descend from apes. The question is, what will we descend to?

To every action, there is an equal and opposite reaction. So said Newton. To every goodness, there is an equal and opposite evil. So said…

Money is the root of all evil? Not necessarily. But evil is the root of most money.

In this society, there are two main groups of people: one group is busy creating evidence, the other group is equally busy in suppressing the evidence.

To scientists, silence is not golden, but evidence is.

What is the point of giving a eulogy when the dead is not listening?

Regulations and laws are not without loopholes. Some people are especially employed or highly paid just to look for them.

Etiquette is an old code of conduct. It does not seem to work anymore.

It is not that he thinks little of others, he just happens to think too much of himself.

Don't believe that men are all equal in the eyes of law; some are still more equal than others… whether you like it or not.

Say Something More

The funny thing is we only meet almost all our close and distant relatives during funerals, especially the patriarch's or matriarch's funeral. Why can't we meet at a happier time?

What a terrible time those people must have spent in order to strive for a good time!

One often hears that time and tide wait for no man. However, this does not necessarily have any impact on the very rich and powerful.

The difference between antique furniture and old furniture is that the former is the prerogative of the rich and the latter the only possession of the poor.

Why think or bother about the future, since most of us are without any future?

The words 'gambol' and 'gamble' have the same pronunciation. One is joyful play and the other a risky adventure. Somehow, marriage is sandwiched between them.

By and large, the future will have nothing in store for you if you are not storing for the future now.

It is quite ironic that the person who thinks most about the future is the one who has nothing to live for in the present.

There is no future in anything. The future is what you are now.

Man and woman are distinguished by their attitudes toward the future: a woman will fear the future before marriage, while a man will fear the future after marriage.

Nobody can gamble with life better than one who is penniless.

Games are strange things: when you watch them, you are relaxing; when you play them, you are exercising; and when you work at them, you are earning a living.

Isn't this paradoxical? You exercise hard to lose weight, but you eat more after the hard exercise.

The word 'generalisation' has two meanings: one leads to a sweeping statement, the other ends up with a scientific principle.

Seldom are women that generous, only perhaps on the occasions when they lavishly give other women away.

The world loves geniuses, but not all geniuses love the world.

Geniuses normally don't see eye to eye, so there should not be more than one genius in each profession or field of study.

Genius is not a lifelong possession. Some have it briefly, others manage to keep it longer.

You may need talent to excel in sports, nevertheless you must have genius to outshine others in science.

Whether one likes it or not, talent is simply not equatable to genius. A genius is always talented in some ways, but a talented person is not necessarily a genius.

Blessed are the ones who know they are blessed.

It appears that only the rich seem to know better how the poor suffer. The poor themselves hardly know they are suffering.

What is she, an Asian, Eurasian or European? She wears black hair one day, blonde hair the next day and red hair the third.

The funny thing is that people seem to blush less and less nowadays. Either the skin is getting thicker or the blood vessels do not show up at all.

Some people will brag about how little they know about something; others will be equally loud at bragging about something they hardly know.

The only virtue of a braggart, if there is any, is that he does not talk about others. Unfortunately few braggarts even possess that virtue.

A boaster is a great inventor. He invented his own stories.

It is fine for us to have two eyes and two ears. However, I think most of us have one mouth too many. One may as well born without a mouth and feed through the nose.

Yes, the pot calls the kettle black. And it screams through its spout when it is boiling.

Man only began to learn to fear man more and more half a century ago, when the nuclear bomb was invented.

We tend to lose the strength of our backbones faster nowadays, ever since heavy loads have been carried around by machines.

The higher you go, the faster and heavier you will fall. This may be true in physics, but need not be applicable in sociology.

Ever trusted a fortune-teller? Never, for two reasons: the fortune-teller does not know his own fortune, and you are solely responsible for your own fortune.

Say What You Think

Censors are a group of very privileged people. They read what others cannot read, and they see what others cannot see.

If you have nothing better to do, be a censor – all you need is a pair of scissors.

'The most incomprehensible thing about the world is that it is comprehensible,' Einstein remarked. It is fine for Einstein to utter that, but certainly not you or me.

The word 'star' when spelt backward is 'rats'. Obviously stars are not rats in the metaphorical sense of the word, though some are closer to it than others.

The optimist would say, 'If winter is around the corner, can spring be far away?'
The pessimist would reply, 'I am not even sure if I can sail through this bitter winter, let alone look forward to the faraway spring.'

A father tells his son, 'When I was your age, I did not behave the way you do.'
The son curtly answers, 'When I am your age, I'll say the same thing to my son.'

The two ends of a circle always meet, no matter where they are – except the ends of the wheel of fortune.

In big cities, cinemas are ideal places for the loners as

well as the lovers.

The mass media are a curse. We are subtly and unconsciously transformed into zombies, and still thank the media for providing us the entertainment.

The world is definitely changing. A century ago, some fathers would not be very sure who all their children are. Nowadays, a child would be equally unsure who their father or fathers are.

What is the difference between a city and a village? There are lots of people, including lots of lonely people, in the city; while there are much fewer people and hardly any lonely people in the village.

The progress of civilisation is directly proportional to the killing power of military weapons. When reaching a critical point, the direct proportion plunges to become a very steep inverse proportion.

Man started in a cave, and will one day end up in cave too – an underground shelter.

Many women change their minds as often as (if not more than) their clothes – not to offer any new idea but to reflect an unsettled mind.

Many politicians say many smart things. If they were to write down all that they said, the word 'literature' would have to be redefined.

Women are not a rare species, half of the world's population are women – yet why is it that they are so difficult to understand?

From women's point of view, men exist to assist them

and nothing else.

Freud once said, 'After all these years of research, I still do not know what a woman wants.' Does anybody know?

Witnesses in the court of law are funny creatures. They sometimes suddenly forget what they always remember, and at other times they suddenly remember things they have long forgotten or that never happened.

What is the difference between a scientist and a philosopher? A scientist will look at the consistency of events, whereas a philosopher will ponder over their inconsistencies.

A witty person needs not be wise, but a wise person will know what wit is.

We always look forward to the day when we get things we have been wanting. After a short euphoria about getting what we wanted, we will ask ourselves why on earth we wanted the things at all.

A needy want is desirable, a lavish want is greedy, and an impossible want is avaricious.

Our needs are countable, but our cravings are countless.

The chance of a wise man making a blunder is equal to that of an idiot achieving success. And remember, the chance has a numerical value between 0 and 1.

You can only be truly wise if you dare to be a fool once in a while.

He is wise who learns more from his enemies than his friends.

This world does not need any more smart people now; it needs more wise ones.

Do not undervalue what small children may have to say. Sometimes what they say may even make the so-called wise people blush.

Wisdom is not what you think. It is other people thinking what you think.

The Chinese believed there were four vices in men: women, wine, gambling and drugs. The four vices of men today are still women, wine, gambling and drugs – the wrappings may have altered here and there, but the contents remain the same.

Don't call an old man smart. A really smart old man should be respected and addressed as wise old man.

A watch is a watch because it keeps people watching it all the time.

A watch keeps itself very busy by moving its hands non-stop.

It is said that a person is judged by the clothes he is wearing. How then would one judge those men who all wear similar ties and coats every day? Not only that, a guard may be in a smart and expensive uniform, while a smart professor may be just wearing a jumper for a stroll on the beach.

Women may not be accurate observers of events, but they are certainly superb observers of fashion.

Don't assume that women wear pretty clothes to attract men; more often than not they do so to ensure other women do not out-wear them.

Some women make clothes to reveal their curves; some clothes make women hide their lines.

Many a woman buys more and more clothes so that she can wear less and less.

Tea breaks are getting more taxing; you work much harder through loud but trivial chatting.

Having a cold is not so bad; having a cold shoulder from those near to you can be much worse.

This cold virus is real naughty. You need about four days to have it cured by taking medicine, and it cures itself in the same number of days.

If you think the cold war is already history and was really bad, wait till you get a hot war.

The United Nations was a lame duck, ignored totally by the Western powers during the Kosovo crisis. It is also a dumb and numb lamb, dumped by the Russians in the Chechen debacle.

A university degree is no guarantee to any success in the future. It all depends on (a) what kind of university it is, and (b) what sort of degree it is.

What good is a university education when school leavers are claiming that they already know what they want to know?

A little knowledge is dangerous. This is exactly what a great many universities and colleges are trying to give their students.

If a young man can earn enough money within a year to see him through a three-year university programme, he will probably have learnt more than the programme could offer.

How often do university graduates get employed by graduate employers? Chances are the employers will be university dropouts who have had a few years' head start.

Some of us detest colours, more so when people are being indiscriminately discriminated against for their skin colour.

Does any politician ever realise that he is no better than a comedian in action? If he did, he would likely stop being a politician.

Most comedians are men. Women simply refused to be laughed at.

Man and woman come from different species. A woman will put on a new dress, no matter how uncomfortable it is; a man will go for comfortable clothing, no matter how old it is.

A fisherman catches fish and sells them, whereas an angler may not be able to catch any fish so he buys them – the former earns his livelihood, the latter spends his.

Anglers are envied not because they have special skills in fishing, but because they seem to have endless leisure.

An angler may boast about the size of the fish he caught; one wonders if fish ever boast about the size of the angler they escaped from.

A lover is like an angler. All he needs is time, patience and some bait.

A fish gets caught only because it opens its mouth too often and too much.

Asking question like 'Which came first, the chicken or the egg?' is just like asking why the sky must be blue and not green – questions of no consequence.

Fire can get out of control easily for it does not know what it is doing. Likewise anger; it is no better than fire.

A finance company is one which will offer you a loan to cover another loan.

If you have not tasted any misery in life, try getting loans from several finance companies.

A person who is always pointing fingers at others has had little opportunity to offer his hands.

Sayings, More Sayings

Do not teach the crab how not to walk sideways. To the crab, sideways is straightforward. There is no such word as sideways in its dictionary. There is in ours, though.

If all the monkey can think of is monkey business, why try and change its thinking?

Never attempt to reveal all the secrets of the universe. A bare and completely exposed universe would not be thrilling anymore.

Sodium is extremely active and corrosive. Chlorine is poisonous and harmful. But when the two meet, the result is a wonderful product which we consume everyday. So, the mathematicians have been right: the product of two negatives is a positive.

This is a paradox: animals which have hardly any reasoning power do not seem to make any mistake in their lives. They live by instinct. But we, the ones possessing the greatest reasoning power of all animals, make mistakes every day.

What makes us think that bees are busy and work harder than us? Each bee may make only a trip to the flowers a day. When we see bees frequenting different flowers at different times of the day, they may not be the same bees. All the bees look alike to us, and this gives rise to the misconception.

Eggs are smarter than we think. They know precisely how to make use of the animals to produce another egg of their kind to perpetuate themselves.

All things are just superficial. So do not read too deep into them lest you may be disappointed.

God is not meant to be perceived by the eyes or brain; God can only be seen by the heart. If that is the case, we all have a god of our own.

The greatest inventions in the whole history of mankind are 'heaven and hell'.

Never try to analyse a person. If you do, be prepared to accept the darkest side of human nature.

'Man is the most intelligent animal.' Who said that? Not the apes, nor the flies nor the frogs, but man himself.

How strange it is for man to have an almost infinite capability and capacity for telling lies, yet at the same time remain unperturbed and insensitive in doing so.

We are conscious of our images in the mirror. Will the images be likewise conscious of our existence?

Catch the golden moment when the first approaching light chases away the dark night, that is, the very instant before the swarms of hatred, lies, intolerance and jealousy pollute the world.

It is believed that when God created this world and humans, God said it was good. I wonder if God is still around today and looking at the world and humans again. Would God still say it is good?

Many years ago, we might have said, 'That is incredible, it could not be true' and got away with it unscathed. Would we want to say the same thing again in the face of modern science and high technology nowadays?

We often think that those things we work for but are unable to get are more beautiful or valuable than others. However, once we get them, our sense of value changes, and we do not think them as beautiful or valuable anymore.

Its not that man is not intelligent. The stupid, more often tragic, thing is that most of us want to believe that we are intelligent, and hence refuse to admit we are not intelligent.

Life is basically dynamic. Imagine what would happen if your heart decided to go static and take a rest, albeit a very short one.

The most ironical thing in life is that we know it is almost impossible to conquer our desires, yet we labour day and night trying to satisfy these insatiable desires.

For someone who is consistently drowned in unfathomable fear, everything appears to be ghastly and threatening. This is one of the worst traumas in life.

Fear not, but kill not too.

Anger associates itself with destruction, while love

helps to build in a subtle way.

He who is incensed with uncontrollable anger burns himself irrevocably.

Never try to argue sensibly with an angry person, for he is more a beast than a human.

Do not ever look into a mirror when you are angry. You would not recognise the ugly animal in the mirror.

Needs and necessities save us from the embarrassments and hassles of choice.

The best way out of a dilemma is not to have got into one in the first place. But the darn fact is we could not know when a dilemma would not be a dilemma.

For many of us, right and wrong are all messed up, especially for muddle-headed people or those madly in love.

Lao-tze said, 'Tao cannot be named, whatever can be named is not Tao.' This seems to be contradictory. Isn't Tao itself already a name? If Tao is not a name, what is it? A concept, a word, a nothing or something indescribable? Even something indescribable is a name. After all, his 'name' and my 'name' are different 'names'.

Sun-tze said, 'Know your enemy and assess your own ability, you will win 100 times in 100 battles.' I would say, 'Know your wife and know yourself, you will be lucky to win 50 times in 100 arguments.'

Sun-tze said, 'Hit your enemy hard when they are at

their weakest.' Is this not tantamount to bullying? Has it got anything to do with smart logistics? Yet it becomes a maxim among people in trade and commerce.

Never believe in any autobiography. It is what the author thinks now about his past.

And if an autobiography is often smeared with pretences, what about biographies, especially memoirs!

Temptations wait to pounce on the young but avoid the old. The old are too weak to be attracted by strong temptations.

Lots of people have axes to grind. They are not grinding because they just cannot find the right grinders at the right time.

Women tend to think that their husbands are their babies, more so when they cannot have any more of their own.

Nowadays it is fine for men to remain bachelors. After all, there are so many willing cohabitant partners waiting around.

Can a bachelor's life be that bad? No, not any more in this modern era. In any case, if life as a single is that bad, imagine life as a double.

It is not that a bachelor does not love a woman, it is just that he loves himself more.

The difference between a bachelor and a married man is that the former may have been crossed once, but the latter is usually double-crossed.

Bankruptcy and economy are the two sides of a see-saw, one goes up when the other goes down.

A bankrupt is not poor but smart. He puts all his money in his trousers and lets people take his apparently more valuable coat.

'Look before you leap' – so goes a wise saying. This is not true anymore; modern young people tend to look only after they have leapt, and are not even bothered where they might have landed.

If you believe everything the advertisements say, you are no better than your ancestors believing in the power of the monkey god.

Man who know how to advertise themselves well in front of ladies may win their hands one day. Unfortunately such relationships seldom last. Advertisements tend to lose their lustre fast.

Here is an ancient Chinese saying: 'Those who know do not talk, those who talk do not know.' This is certainly out of context now, otherwise where would the teachers, lecturers, salespersons and consultants find their jobs?

Do not be over-awed by new theories in the social sciences, chances are they are just old wines in new bottles.

Overheard from a person leaving a new product sale promotion seminar: 'Lies, more lies, nothing but lies!'

Imagine spending $500 to attend a heavily advertised one-day seminar-cum-workshop run by some supposedly high-strung well-groomed speakers, and end up with yourself more disillusioned than ever.

Why talk so much about bikinis, when there is actually nothing much left to talk about?

Avoid flatterers by all means, unless of course you like to live above the clouds and are ready to fall flat.

Time is the greatest justice of all. When the time has come, no one will be spared – even if you are powerful, rich, famous or beautiful.

Money cannot buy time? No, it can. Money can bail you out of jail and wait for appeal after appeal.

Can money buy conscience? Can and cannot. It all depends whether you have one or none.

Beauty is more than skin deep, it is sin shallow.

Marketing is begging in disguise, though it is a smart one at that.

Man strives for shorter time and more money. Would bees strive for a shorter line and more honey?

Computers compute. Man manoeuvres. But never let computers compute to out-manoeuvre man.

Information is not knowledge. Information downloaded from a computer is just like the contents of a book. You have to learn and digest before you can call it your knowledge.

When life becomes too easy-going, we abuse it unknowingly. As soon as information becomes too easy to access, we abuse it to make it cheap.

Cultures are not meant to be assessed, whatever the context in which the assessment may take place.

There is no such thing as superior culture, no culture should supersede another. They are supposed to be complementary.

When we talk, we think we talk sense. When others talk, we think they talk nonsense.

How many of us would always want to be the audience? We want to be the main actor or speaker, at least some of the time if not most of the time.

Could it be true that the commencement of old age is not the beginning of an end? If not, then it must be the end of a beginning.

North poles attract south poles, and positive charges never fail to attract negative charges. In marriage, this may not be always true. Opposite sexes attract each other at the beginning but repel as time passes.

If you still think you can raise your children like your parents did, then be prepared to face a time bomb.

People tend to believe the unbelievable because they have no explanation for the impossible.

If you believe everything a private medical practitioner says, you are not as healthy as you think; and if you believe everything a preacher says, you are not as sinless as you wish to be.

Sinful are the people who indulge in excessive gossiping and exaggerate stories out of context, out of proportion.

A good friend may turn out to be your worst enemy, for he knows when and where to attack your weakest side.

Some Insights

To maintain a harmonious family, parents would have to treat their children as guests and the children would have to treat their parents as hosts.

A harmonious family begins with mutual respect, the mutual respect of each and every member of the family.

If you two people cannot stand each other, then just sit down instead of showdown.

Contain your hatred. If not, it may just start with a spark and end up in a wild fire.

What is the point of having a head when the mind stops functioning?

How do you fancy a person who thinks with the heart but loves with the brain?

A woman's world view starts at the heart and ends in the brain; the man's is exactly the other way round.

How many of us would want to trade all our wealth for our good health?

To keep a healthy heart and a sound mind, avoid anger, hatred and jealousy.

If you keep thinking of what other people are thinking about, you are not thinking.

And if you think along the same line as others do, you are still not thinking.

Only a few people actually think; others think they think, and the rest do not know if they are thinking.

It is a criminal waste of time to think about what other people are thinking about you.

Many a young man is like a hypothesis, he has to grow old to confirm his hypothesis.

The best explanation of 'heaven and hell' is there is no explanation.

Temptation may be hard to resist when it knocks on your door, but you can still learn how not to open the door.

Temptation can come in many different disguises; you need to be constantly prepared to dispel it each time by having the right mind-set and right thinking.

Temper only surfaces when it is lost – so keep your temper with care.

If you cannot find heaven on earth, then chances are you will find earth in heaven.

The person who praises heaven most often is the one who is least keen to go now.

Heaven is a terrible misconception, hell is worse.

Why create a heaven and a hell outside our physical beings when many of us know too well that they are all the time hiding inside us?

To most people, a lie is heaven and truth is hell.

Many friends will come to offer their moral support in your times of difficulty; you may wonder if there will be anyone to give you financial support.

Many friends will remain friends only when they will not have to go out of their way to help you.

Do not forget, you help others to help yourself, sometime, somehow.

Make way for others, the world will be wide and spacious.
Smile at one another, all else will be calm and fine.
Say a word less, the atmosphere will be more tranquil.
Tolerate nonsense here and there, the world is not as dark as you think.

With good heredity, you have had a head start; your achievement then lies in your own effort and environment.

If everyone is a hero or heroine, who is there to clap at you on stage?

How often do we laugh at ostriches burying their heads in the sand and not realising that we are in no way better than they are?

Everyone has wonderful and clear vision with hindsight, while the vision for foresight (if any) is always cloudy and blurred.

Almost all of us become smart in retrospect; we always claim we knew that was going to happen beforehand.

History repeats itself – this is the greatest mistake of mankind.

Rightly so, history is his (a historian's) story – not yours or mine.

The only thing we learn from history is that we learn nothing from history.

Are we not running around in spirals trying to make ends meet?

If we do run around in circles, the ends will meet somehow but the routine is boring many of us to death.

To keep a family going, what we need are warm hearts and not hot heads.

Temperature is a measure of the degree of hotness. A cool family is not cold, it is a family of cool heads.

If we are not careful, we may become victims of television in the near future.

Most of the time, watching TV enslaves the mind. It does not make us think, instead it prompts us to accept what it offers.

The impact of TV on children's minds is so deep and powerful that you will be surprised how children change their attitudes and behaviour.

If you think talk is cheap, just look at the telephone bill for long-distance calls.

When Bell invented the telephone, he did not mean it to be used for long gossips.

A modern kid may be defined as someone who talks over the phone, watches TV and with one ear attached to an earphone of a CD player – all at the same time.

One can have faith in science and technology ushering in a grand new era for mankind, but one can be destroyed by science and technology in a subtle way.

This is flabbergasting: very often we pay for being honest, but we get paid for being dishonest.

Surely you cannot be serious about honesty being the best policy? It is simply not true anymore.

To be honoured and yet not deserving the honour is common everywhere; there is no need for anyone to be unduly alarmed.

Hope may be redefined as expecting something for nothing. Still, it is better to keep the hope alive than lose all hope in life.

If you are greedy, blame human nature. If you are deceptive, blame human nature. If you are hypocritical, blame human nature again.

Man has appeared to have conquered nature in a big way, but has never been successful in conquering human nature.

Indeed, the human race has come to a critical point in evaluating whether we are leading in the race for human survival or being left far behind.

Many of us shun humility, thinking it is a bitter swallowing of self-pride. How many of us would have thought that people who can stand humility without losing any pride are the truly great people?

When hunger starts gnawing at your vitals, you not

only lose your vitality, but also your sensibility.

Truth cannot be bought or sold, but in this world of commerce, it can be traded at a market value.

When trouble begins to trouble you, resist with all your might the trouble that is troubling you.

Never tell people your troubles, they either listen to you casually or are glad that they are not in the same shoes.

A friend who wants to share your troubles is a true friend indeed.

A tourist sees what others want him to see; a traveller sees what he wants to see.

A traveller travels light, a tourist equips himself with unnecessary gear.

A tourist sees new things at a glance, a traveller searches his soul through observation of foreign cultures.

Good translation of literature is rare. It is better to read it in its original language. If that is not possible, then ensure that the translation reflects the spirit of the literature and not just its literal interpretation.

Why do most dramas end in tragedy? Is it because the audience can then leave the theatre feeling more fortunate than others?

How can man be so stupid as to invent traffic jams? They're a criminal waste of time and energy.

Has anyone ever estimated the man-hours lost in

traffic jams or the related slowdown of vehicles due to heavy traffic in the cities all over the world? Would you be surprised if I tell you that it is more than 100 million man-hours per working day?

To say 'thank you' is meant to be polite and grateful. However, the two words have been repeated so often, day in and day out, that they have lost their original meaning. I doubt how many people really mean to thank you when they say 'thank you'.

Gratefulness and gratitude are heavy emotional burdens, that is why it is always better to give than take.

Truly great people don't just become great, they are great by themselves.

Indeed, some people achieve greatness, some are born to be great and others become great by sheer luck and circumstance.

Greed is an eternal curse. It burns people, old and young.

Tomorrow has not ended, it will never end. So why wait till tomorrow when you can get things done today?

Tolerance cannot be a virtue anymore, especially when the oppressor tells the oppressed to be tolerant.

Time is the greatest impartial judge, it leaves no hair unwhitened.

When you were young time killed you; now you are old you kill time.

When time kills you, you find it slipping by far too fast; when you kill time, it does not seem to move at all.

Lightning and thunder occur simultaneously; and because lightning is much faster, it gets to inform you first.

Telling the poor to be frugal is worse than adding salt to the wound.

It is much better to have one thought at a time than to have many thoughts all the time.

A second thought may not necessarily be a better thought, for it often contradicts the first thought.

The haves will thirst for fame, the have-nots for money, leaving the most unfortunate ones thirsting for clean water.

How many of us will say that we are devoid of any guilt at the last moment of our lives?

Like good people, good habits die young; and the bad habits persist.

About 1% of world people make things happen, 30% follow what has happened, and the remaining 69% do not know what is happening.

Happiness is a mental state; it all happens in the mind.

The more you share your happiness, the happier you are.

Only share your happiness with others, but never your sufferings.

The secret to a happy life is never keep any secret.

Happiness comes from making other people happy.

There is no real happiness in this world; it is up to you to determine your own happiness.

Speak Out

A smart person knows when to act and when not to act. A smarter person knows when and how to act, and when and how not to act. The smartest person understands when, how and what to act, and when, how and what not to act.

Try not to ask a favour from anyone if you can, lest one day you find yourself burdened by favours you cannot shoulder.

Some people seem to have an insatiable appetite. Give them a millimetre, they want a centimetre. Give them a centimetre, they ask for a metre. After being granted their wish for a metre, they demand everything you have.

We can be nice to some people once, we can still be nice to the same people twice. How many of us would want to be nice to them more than thrice if there is no reciprocation?

We should count our blessings. The world has given many of us more than we deserve.

Ignorance can be bliss, provided it has nothing to do with earning a living.

There are three five-letter words we must all avoid at all cost in life: *greed*, *anger*, and *covet*.

For some people like me, it may be easy to study physics and mathematics, but quite impossible to learn the intricacies and subtleties of human relationships. No book can be written containing the myriads of individual idiosyncrasies of the six billion people on earth.

The United States is now the only world superpower. Absolute power intoxicates. Will the US be so intoxicated and euphoric in its accomplishment that it will one day deny the rights of other countries in the twenty-first century?

A friendship can be made and broken and remade; marriage cannot.

The alarm clock is the most taxing instrument ever invented; it has been taxing my nerves almost every dawn for more than forty-five years.

Words are powerful; they are certainly mightier than the sword if used properly. They are only that powerful when they are concise, precise, and right at the point.

How often will corruption at the top bring down a government? – Not so often now, especially with all the smart people from different professions acting insidiously and collaboratively.

There is a bright side to everything, except that the other side is always dark.

Talking About That

'If I have seen further it is by standing on the shoulders of giants.' Newton is supposed to have made this brilliant statement. We are nowhere near Newton, but perhaps we can at least try to make some bold hypothesis and strive to prove it in our own way. We can stand on the shoulders of dwarfs, for a start.

In life, we cannot always be in a win-win situation. What is wrong if we do lose now and then?

Do not be so naïve as to think that only the best man wins. This is often not the case. Moreover, the best man is there to support the morale of the bridegroom.

One of the elements of success is a strong will. However, not all children will appreciate this kind of will; they look forward to another kind as you are getting old.

Blessed is the man who has a wife who sees him through thick and thin throughout his life – that is, through thick and thin.

A married man often dreams of his former girlfriend, thinking she is still as sweet and pretty as she was until they chance upon each other again one day. This applies to a married woman too.

If only a spouse could see more of the virtues than the weaknesses of the other half, married life could be more wonderful.

Rich and elderly men marry young girls, and the smart men follow closely behind to marry the widows.

The world is getting crazy, there are so many happy young widows around.

A drunkard is a brave man; he does what others dare not and lives to regret it later.

A commercial aims to attract people, but its hidden aim is to distract them as much as possible.

A committee is a special group of people whose main purpose is to look for a victim to carry out their instructions.

Many executives like to sit on committees, especially when their main task is to chair the meetings – for some other people will be charged with the onerous task of doing the donkey work.

How many people would not mind airing their grand opinions in a committee meeting, but shy away from implementing their proposals themselves?

A lot of us have a lot of common sense, the trouble is how many of us know how to put it into practice?

To many people, common sense is not common, neither is it sense; they cannot make sense out of things that are so common.

Don't send me a letter addressed 'To whom it may concern', I am not in the least concerned with such an all-in-one addressee.

Never mind whatever systems you may have in politics, you always end up with an oppressing individual or group manipulating the majority oppressed group. Even democracy is not entirely democratic when you come to the question of power.

Here is an old Chinese adage: 'Choose someone your superior to be your friend.' On the surface it appears to be wise. However, it is simply illogical. If someone superior to you goes by these words, he would not befriend you in the first place.

A person is known by the company he keeps. On the other hand, would the company be known by the person they keep? They may just be his followers or cronies.

Never compare two persons in any way unless you have a definite benchmark and objectivity to begin with. How often do we fall into the trap of such comparison when there is indeed nothing to compare?

Never compare what you have with what you deserve. Such a comparison is meaningless because you do not necessary deserve what you think you deserve.

A person's life is compensated in a very strange way. Rich people may have lots of money but no child, whereas poor people may have lots of children but no money.

The person who complains most about life is the person who works the least.

Think, Think

When our children are grown-ups, it does not mean that our worries end there. Do not be surprised to find yourself having more worries.

Just ignore people who tell you not to worry and ask what there is to worry about. There is nothing wrong in a little worry, it's a natural psychological reaction to unhappy or unsettling events around you. This is how you find your energy to pull yourself together to face yet another day.

Of course, too much undue and constant worry will flatten you in no time.

Do not expect too much from the world. Take it as it is, and not what you think it should be.

The world is a stage. Why is it not putting on good shows for everyone?

Travel around to see the world whenever you can. The more you come to understand it the better prepared you are for the next one (if there is a next one).

Life is like a mirror. Smile, and it smiles at you; cry, and it cries too. And the world is your life.

God does not seem to have made this world a fine one. He was probably in a hurry and put his sketches to work.

Can the world get better or worse? No, it just keeps spinning.

It is not that the world gets better or worse, it is humankind that does.

Man egotistically assumes that he is destined to mend all the ills of this world, when he knows darn well he cannot.

A workaholic is not a dull person, he is his boss's gleaming gem.

Which would you choose? To live without working, or to work without living?

It is the amount of work you put in a day that matters, not the other way round.

Procrastination is the curse of routine work, it makes work too cheap.

The other four-letter word which spells life is work.

One's achievement is determined not so much by one's labour, but more by one's intelligence – any kind of intelligence.

A man who does not speak a single word is either a sage or a moron – whichever comes first.

There's More to Words than Just Words

Man is said to be the ultimate product of evolution (or if you prefer, the gem of God's creation). Man is the only animal that talks, and an ass does not talk. But somehow, many people talk like as if asses are talking. I wonder how; I don't know why.

Beware, ladies and gentlemen. Do not get prosperous and famous overnight, chances are you will turn preposterous the following night.

Actions naturally speak louder than words, especially when there are fewer lies to tell.

Empty vessels sound loud in a different way, most notably when the vessel is made up of meaningless words.

Women are inexplicable creatures: not only they are very expensive to get, but also they become more expensive to hold; and worst of all, they will be beyond your means to drop. I am perplexed.

How I envy women: they have an infinite capacity for accepting praise and gifts, but will explode at the slightest insinuation of insult. Well, most men are no better.

Most women are great thinkers: when a woman is not thinking about herself, she will be thinking whether other people are thinking about her.

Blessed is a lady who knows when to talk and when not to. If you meet a lady of this kind, marry her even if she is not pretty, lest you get entangled with a sharp-tongued and nagging woman later.

What? You think apples are costly nowadays? Do you know how much the apple in the Garden of Eden cost? Never mind if you are a non-Christian.

Marriage is a risk. It is not even a calculated risk. It is an adventure, an experience which leads to the path of no return.

Don't be mislead by the act of the seemingly loving couple in public. How often are they tearing at each other's faces in private?

All of us are liars to some extent; the difference is one of degree and not of kind. Nowadays the worst and most blatant lies are told by advertisements.

You cannot stop time by stopping your watch. Likewise, you cannot stop rampant lies by telling more lies.

Don't act smart by throwing your advice around everywhere. To those people who know, your advice will be empty and useless; and to those who do not know, your advice will carry no meaning either.

If a person swears that his word is as good as his honour, then question his honour first.

You won't have to eat too many of your own words if you haven't talked too much.

Useless words are aplenty, right and wise words few.

He who laughs last laughs best. He who speaks last speaks best too.

No one will have a chance to hit back at the person who speaks last.

Pity the lecturer who has to use so many words to talk about so few things – but then he is paid by the number of words he says.

The very sight of a waterfall enlightens one's heart. But it would be more enlightening if the water did not fall.

A beautiful lady may not be charming, but a charming woman is certainly pretty.

The main bulk of a newspaper may be divided into three sections – trivial and sensational news, still trivial news, and more sensational news.

What can be more annoying than a chatterbox? Another chatterbox.

A chatterbox is someone who just cannot stop talking until forced to do so by your abrupt departure.

A con man is someone who is always busy – busy looking for his victims.

No one would be able to con any one else if man wasn't so greedy – stupendously greedy.

Bank cheques have duped people to believe that their signatures are worth millions, that is, millions on paper.

If you see a person smile while he's doing something

alone, a happy thought must have just flashed across his mind. Such is a cheerful person.

The strange thing is why there are eight pawns and one queen in a chess game. Why not the other way round? Indeed, who wants to be a pawn in any game at all? Everyone wants to be a queen.

Children are often in an awkward, no-win situation. When they are too noisy, they get reprimanded; and when they're too quiet, they get sent to a clinic.

How many parents can claim that they know child psychology when all they know is hearsay childish psychology?

A child psychologist would find it hard to bring up his own children, for he often finds that theory and practice do not go hand in hand – his children are his own very image and likeness.

A child psychologist seems to understand most about any children other than his own.

Children are a happy-go-lucky lot. They do not know how to recall their past, neither do they care about their future.

Happy are those who treasure their present, and are oblivious to their past and future.

Nothing can make a childless couple more irritated and frustrated than the cry of the neighbour's newborn baby.

Don't be coaxed into believing that children can be raised by the book. No book will contain the facts on how to deal with the idiosyncrasies of every child.

We are the obliging people, inclined to say 'yes' more than 'no'. There are times in life when we have to be firm and be abrasive enough to say 'no', especially to our children while they are still young.

If we give our small children too many 'yes's, they will give us as many 'no's when they grow up.

To working parents, time is money. But do not trade time for money with your children; what they need is more of your time than money.

A genius can be talented, but a talented person need not necessarily be a genius.

It takes a genius to differentiate between genius and talent, but someone talented would think it otherwise.

A gentleman needs not be truly gentle: he may be just gentle in appearance and not at heart.

There is a subtle art in giving: give a girl something she looks pretty in, and give a boy something which sweetens his mouth.

Presents not only make hearts grow fonder, they make faces more radiant.

Girls are generally beautiful, so to speak; and they are beautiful, so to speak generally.

Thoughtful Statements

Fashion is like waves, it repeats itself in cycles.

Fashion seems to have penetrated all walks of life. Have you not heard of fashionable cars, fashionable food, fashionable ideas, fashionable words, fashionable toys…?

Crime does not pay? No. It gets paid in drama and TV series.

Capital punishment is not carried out by the law. It is man entrusted with legality who ends another person's life.

It appears to be so much easier to be a critic than the professional under criticism.

Give a critic his due, credit him for the imbecility of his words.

Never challenge a critic's viewpoints, unless you want to be further critiqued.

You don't have to be a learned person to be a critic, all you need is the skill of word manipulation, egotism, egotism, and egotism.

A large crowd is the best place to incite mob psychology; you will be surprised how spontaneously they will go along with you.

We seem to have more street protests in this high

technology era. One wonders whether people protest because they have a genuine reason, or because they see TV cameras all around them.

Somehow the public have been gradually seduced by the mass media to such an extent that the subtle influence has become a subconscious affair.

People used to think that marriage is the best medicine for a love affair. This has changed. Marriage is now the bitter medicine for many love affairs.

Curiosity not only kills the cat, it kills everyone if overstretched.

'Things were different in the past, they are not the same now.' Things change, we change too.

The only consistent thing about things is the inconsistencies of things.

The shortest distance between any two points is not always a straight line. Like the geodesic on a spherical surface, the curve is the shortest line.

Aesthetically speaking, a curve is certainly more charming than a plain line.

Perhaps I may be more of a cynic than anything else, as I tend to see things from their darker side.

Joyous is the person who dances to the tune of everyone else.

A public speaker is someone who knows a little of almost everything, and comprehends nothing of everything.

It is not that a little knowledge is dangerous. It is the person who knows little that is dangerous.

Occasional daydreaming is fine. It helps to keep your mental state in balance.

The last thing a person ever wants to have is the last thing he or she has – death.

To some, death is the ultimate end; to others, it is only yet another beginning.

A person without a debt or loan of any kind is a truly free person.

Some people say war is a prelude to peace. Does that mean peace is likewise a prelude to war?

The twentieth century will go down in history as the bloodiest century, in consequence of two world wars plus numerous battles.

In time of peace, children would weep at their parents' graves; in war, the parents would play their children's role.

In order to stop all these senseless killings in wars once and for all, have another world war.

No one will have time to think about whether or not the war has been right; the only concern is who are left.

Each medal on the general's chest was earned at the expense of thousands of lives of the soldiers and civilians.

How paradoxical! Killing a person is a capital crime,

while killing thousands of enemies is a glorious action.

In war, you pay for everything: you pay for the ammunition and weapons, you pay for the generals and soldiers, and you pay for your family's and your own lives.

Try not to keep people waiting, unless of course, you are prepared to wait for them even longer.

Some people think that if they wait long enough, they will eventually get what they want – including death.

You must be really getting old when you only look at the food you get in a restaurant and don't even glance at the attractive waitress.

If you never ask where your spouse has been and are reluctant to accompany her anywhere she goes, then you are certainly an old man.

More and more youngsters are wearing glasses for short-sightedness. At the same time more and more people are putting on tinted glasses. The former wear glasses out of necessity, the latter put on glasses to appease themselves and look at the world in their preferred colour.

A man of vision is a great man, a man of visions is a daydreamer.

Virtue is something to be acted upon and not just thought of. A person of words need not necessarily be a virtuous person.

To many people virginity is to be valued and preserved. In that case, let the virgin forests stay as they are.

Many of us are pawns, pawns to the players on the great world stage. Like the pawns in the chess game, only a few of us are lucky to survive till before the end of the game and be promoted to queens.

In war, surrender is never a virtue; in woman, it is – sort of.

A truly loving spouse is one who overlooks your vice and appreciates your virtue.

How could you convince a fanatic that he is a fanatic? You cannot. The only problem with a fanatic is that he does not even know he is one.

A fanatic has just one conviction – there is no other conviction.

The word 'alternatives' is not in any fanatic's vocabulary.

The marriage institution is fast crumbling, so is the family.

Familiarity breeds contempt. This still holds water, except what a contempt it is now!

Fame is a double-edged, sharp-edged sword. It can propel you sky high and it can reduce you to an obscurity too.

The greatest enemy of fame is time.

When fame comes to you too easily, you will begin to wonder about its genuineness.

There are people who cannot take a stand, because they fall for everything in sight.

Dare to fall, for the experience you gained in a fall is worth ten thousand words.

Well Worded

Avoid asking for anything which is not your due. The trouble with most of us is we take far more often than we give.

The path of craving for illusory glamour leads only to one's downfall.

The existence of supernatural power is not for you to explain, but for you to claim.

It takes a god to understand another god. So, as a layman, do not attempt to comprehend the incomprehensible.

Religion is meant to be believed and trusted, but not questioned.

Religion is an anchor for the faithful, a sanctuary for the disillusioned, and a symbol for the moral upholders.

Essentially all people are good people in this world. They can be divided into three categories: those who are good by conscience, those who are good outwardly, and those who have their own yardstick of goodness.

Never indulge in any form of gossip, lest you want to get yourself burnt first.

Inflated gossip is more poisonous than poison.

Gossip is not gossip if it is not malicious.

The person who carries gossip to you will end up putting you in another piece of gossip.

Rules, constitutions, and laws often do not govern a country – the politicians in power do.

Nowadays, there are just far too many governments of the minority, by the minority, and for the minority.

This seems rather illogical: X thinks that the pasture on the other side of the fence (say Y's) is always greener, and Y likewise thinks that the pasture on this side, X's, is always greener; this means Y>X and X>Y – mathematically impossible.

You can have all the modern cosmetics and plastic surgery to make you look young, but you can never reactivate an ageing mind.

Are you sure whatever goes up must come down? What about age, income tax and the cost of living?

Happy is the person who counts her blessings, sad is the one who counts her age.

A courageous act can be heroic, an equally courageous act can turn into cowardice – it all depends on the circumstances.

How much does conscience weigh? How much is it worth?

It is better to live with your backbone straight and be poor, than to live with your backbone bent and be rich.

How preposterous! Man sells his love and woman sells her desire.

Any girl intending to get married must learn how to resist a man's advance and obstruct his path of retreat.

The person who stoops conquers. Does it mean that a person has to be a coward once in a while?

Man was a creation, woman a recreation – created after the man.

Money is not the most important thing in life anymore. You can still have smart cards, e-cards, credit cards and cash cards.

People in the world of finance can always help you to buy things you do not need. The more you buy the better off they are.

As soon as you ask a favour from someone, get ready to return the same one day.

You need only seconds to detect the faults of others, but you will need a whole lifetime to discover your own.

We are all quick at picking out the mistakes of others, but we are even quicker at hiding our own.

Every father, subconsciously, will want his son to achieve what he himself has inadvertently or inevitably left out in his life.

Do not advise your son to follow your footsteps unless you are doubly certain that they have been the right ones all the time.

Why are we so inclined to advise others on how to bring up their families when our own is starting to crumble?

When we are successful, we attribute it to our own capability. When we fail, we blame our fate.

Throughout human history, the most frequently blamed object has been none other than fate.

In the past, pretty ladies were sources of great joy and comfort to men – until some crazy people with nothing better to do invented fashion.

Do not be lured into buying expensive things just because people say they are fashionable.

What About Physics?

Most physicists are boring people; they bore their audience. As such they tend to make physics boring too.

A good number of physics concepts are rather abstract; they tax students' imagination. The result is many students develop a dislike of physics at an early age.

One way to overcome the abstractness of physics concepts is to 'concretise' them, by doing activities or carrying out simple investigations. Students learn better this way.

Physicists like to build lots of mathematics into physics by playing with formulae after formulae. Not only do the mathematical formulae frighten away students, but they make physics look more mathematics than mathematics itself.

When is physics not mathematics, and when is mathematics not physics? That is the question.

How can one make physics interesting? After almost thirty-five years of teaching and research, I believe the best way is through experiential activities, more experiences and more activities.

Because physics concepts are difficult to grasp, we simplify them at secondary school level. However, oversimplification of concepts tends to make the concepts inaccurate.

Children are pseudo-scientists. They like to form their own views about things happening in their environment and use them to explain various physical phenomena around them. Such preconceptions may blur their concepts about physics and impede their understanding of the right concepts.

Without the effort of the physicists, mathematics would not have been hailed as the queen of science. Or is it more appropriate to call physics the queen of mathematics?

It is quite normal for young people to stay away from physics. The problem is how to make physics attractive to these people.

Physics without mathematics can be quite meaningless. On the other hand, physics with too much mathematics would render physics totally meaningless.

The single amazing property of a photon is that it has a split personality. It will appear as a particle or a wave depending on who the observer is.

A photon appears more comfortable in mathematics than in physics, except in reality its sheer abundance gives us light.

Electrons are said to possess charges. Is an electron a charge, or a charge an electron? What is a charge after all?

Strictly speaking, without its unique property of charge, an electron would be useless.

Modern living is practically impossible without electricity, a continuous flow of charges from the countless number of imperceptible tiny electrons.

If electrons do not behave the way physicists expect

them to, where do we get all these high-technology gadgets and IT?

A single electron is insignificant and of no consequence to anybody. But trillions and zillions of them can move the world.

Do not ignore the power of the electrons and the marvels electrons can bring to mankind. You do so at your own peril.

Neither would you want to underestimate the tremendous and awesome power of electrons. If not properly controlled, they can start a fire to engulf the globe.

Electrons are good servants but bad masters.

A proton possesses an equal and opposite charge to that of an electron. Since unlike charges attract, they tend to move towards each other whenever they meet. As a proton is almost 2,000 times as massive as an electron, the electron dashes forward, nullifying the effect of both charges.

Fortunately, protons and electrons do not see one another that often, and that there are numerous loose or easily detached electrons all over the place to help us to keep our civilisation going. Thanks to them, a sizeable number of people are living lives unimaginable by our ancestors a century ago.

If you think electricity is expensive, try living without it for a day.

Never mind if one day a computer will think like man, the important thing is to make sure that man does not think like a computer of the 1980s.

Technology, coupled with the knowledge of physics, has fast become the new champion of our modern civilisation.

Einstein had been hailed as the greatest thinker of the twentieth century – that makes physics more and more respectable but less and less interesting.

What Else Can I Not Say?

Show us an honest politician, and we shall show you a clean prostitute.

No one stoops so low in front of others as the one waiting to step on their heads.

Of course a picture is worth a thousand words, but only when the picture is done by a professional and the words by an amateur.

An alcoholic always thinks he can drink to forget, but never succeeds in drinking to forget what he thinks.

Someone who agrees with everything you say is either a fool or is trying to make you a fool.

When one grows older, one does not necessary grow wiser, but one becomes more efficient at hiding one's weaknesses and ignorance.

He who is not healthy at thirty, wealthy at forty-five, or wise at sixty, will never live to know what health, wealth or wisdom means.

How this world has changed! Imagine your grown-up children telling you that you are duty-bound to provide what they want, and don't expect them to be perfect because you have not been perfect yourself.

If I'd known that it would be that painful to bring up children, I might have decided to have none. But then, there were other brighter moments.

If I'd known that marriage life would be that tumultuous, I'd have remained a bachelor. But, could I? Would I?

My dear friend, how often have I got to remind you that the world is what you perceive it to be and not what it actually is? Naturally, it would appear dim if you wear dark glasses.

Why does it never occur to you that it would be a waste of energy and time advising someone who is completely blocked by preconceptions and misconceptions to do or think otherwise? Even more so if this someone happens to be your spouse or child. It would be less futile talking to the birds.

The trouble is not with the world. The problem is with you yourself.

Remember, the world owes you nothing, but you owe the world everything. At the very least, your life depends on the well-being of the world.

Every family has its own hidden problem, the problem is when the hidden problem becomes unmanageable and explodes.

I must contain my inner rage, it seems to get uglier.

The word life has four letters. The only two-letter word that can be formed from the four letters is if; well, life is full of ifs. The only three-letter word is lie; yes, life is packed with endless lies. The only other four-letter word from the same four letters is file, indeed, life is loaded with files.

When in a rage, think of space shuttle launching: count 10, 9, 8,… 2, 1, before blasting off.

Beware of anger, it is only a letter 'd' away from danger.

Man is an animal, the most intelligent one at that; yet man feels greatly insulted when called an animal.

How dare you say that as in human society, there is little peace and tranquillity among other animals? At least you can't find lawyers among them.

A neighbour with a noisy old car can be disturbing. But a neighbour with a quiet new posh car is even more upsetting.

The best answer to any question is action.

Not all questions have answers, especially when the questions imply false accusations.

Some people say that we share the same ancestors as the apes. I wonder whether apes have ever thought of that. If they did, what would they say?

An apology is meant to be the right *saying* after a wrong *doing*. Nowadays, how often do we have to apologise for the right things done to the wrong person?

Sincere apologies are hard to come by. More often

than not, they are just beautiful but meaningless words.

Women used to spend lots of time beautifying themselves instead of developing their minds, for they know that most men are idiotic but not blind. While most women still continue making their appearance pretty, many modern men are fast catching up.

Isn't it ironic? A man works hard to make money in his younger days and works equally hard to spend the money when old.

It is funny that a person can agree with someone about something in principle, but would disagree when it comes to actually carrying out the thing.

Arbitration is a dirty job. If an arbitrator settles a dispute between two parties, he will likely be blamed by one of the parties. If he fails, he will be cursed by both.

Do not put your entire trust in a surgeon in a private hospital. Chances are you may be duped into an expensive operation when it is not absolutely necessary. Get a second opinion.

The person who said that archaeologists make good husbands because the older the wives become, the more the husbands are interested in them, has made a serious mistake. Archaeologists do find old things attractive, but only the dead ones.

People fond of arguments share a common weakness: they are quick to dispute things that in fact are indisputable.

Another common denominator of arguers is ignorance. It is just a pity that they refuse to admit their ignorance.

Avoid arguments when possible, more so when they get impossible.

Heated arguments between spouses are really bad. They not only cool your marriage, but also burn your health.

The soundness of an argument varies inversely with its loudness. The louder you talk, the less sound is your argument.

Like a long roll of toilet paper, every argument has two sides, but never seems to have an end.

Do not classify man as good or bad, no matter what the context is. The fact is man is neither good nor bad, just stupid and erratic.

When you do not know what the painting is all about, then it must be modern art.

Not all artists are mad, but most of the really good ones are near insanity.

Want to be an artist? Practically all artists have become famous posthumously, and the value of their works then skyrocketed to millions of dollars; few were as fortunate as Picasso.

I thought I was a free thinker until I realised that I was not supposed to think free.

It's a tragedy. By the time a man knows he can get along without a woman, he is either an invalid or dying.

It is not that an atheist does not believe in God, it is just that he cannot find a suitable one yet.

We take atom-splitting for granted. Soon atoms will take for granted man-splitting.

Marry a beautiful but not so intelligent woman, or a not so beautiful but intelligent one. Never tie the knot with a not so pretty yet stupid woman, nor with a pretty and very intelligent one. Don't ask why.

If all men and women are actors and actresses on a stage, who is the audience?

Wisdom Comes Late

The discovery of electromagnetic induction in the nineteenth century ushered in a new era of scientific activities as well as enhanced the industrial revolution. It triggered the onset of high technology and eventually brought in the age of computers and info-technology.

The British attributed it to Faraday's ingenious experimental work, while the Americans credited it to Henry. How such rivalry in the world of science could turn ethnic was quite intriguing. Indeed, both should be given due credit for the momentous simultaneous independent discovery.

Jealousy and resentment are not uncommon in the world of science. Like others, scientists are still subject to the influence of the darker part of human nature.

Time is the only impartial judge of our final shapes and destinies.

Why has the language related to sex become indecent language? Is it because sex is not taught as a proper subject in school?

Sensuality allows the propagation of the human race, but the overindulgence in sensuality may bring an end to the human race.

If you just count the number of letters, sentimentality

is 64% sentiment and also 64% mentality. It should be 99.9% sentiment and 0.1% mentality.

We are supposed to have five senses, but we never utilise them in full: 90% of us may not have any feelings, 80% may be blind, 70% may be deaf, 60% may be dumb and 50% may not smell.

You may have a sense a humour, but never laugh at others' misadventures.

In many circumstances, the line between sense and non-sense has become so thin that it just fizzles away.

Do not tell someone to try to be more sensible. To many, sensibility is just not learnable or explainable.

The very first day you can laugh at yourself starts the time of your maturity.

An apple a day may not keep the doctor away nowadays, but a laugh a day will surely keep the psychiatrist away.

Poverty is not a disgrace; being dishonestly rich is.

You may be poor, but you do not have to stoop so low because you are poor.

When you begin to laugh at yourself, it is a sure sign that you have matured.

With so many laws and regulations in so many fields, one wonders if it is better to be in a society without such hassles.

A society with minimal regulations and restrictions need not be a lawless society.

Indeed, why would we want laws and rules if we were honest and trustworthy?

In this complex modern society, one can hardly live without a lawyer. What is worse is one cannot die without a lawyer.

Money does not talk all the time, it gets lawyers to talk on its owners' behalf.

It's not that he is lazy, he just needs a good rest before he starts work.

He is lazy, but he thinks he is lucky – he lives much longer than most workaholics.

The world has far too many politicians. What we need are honest and capable leaders.

You do not have to be taught to learn if you have learnt how to learn.

To keep up with the fast changing pace of this high-tech society, we not only have to learn how to access new knowledge, but also to do it as often as we can.

Lifelong education is not a luxury, it has become a necessity.

It is easy to say that we learn from our mistakes, yet how many of us do actually learn from our mistakes in life?

We can learn from anyone. Everyone will know something or possess some skills we do not know, no matter how trivial it may be. The only caution is you have to decide what to learn or what not to learn.

Lecturing is one of the most ineffective ways to impart knowledge; what's more, good lecturers are hard to come by.

It is not too early to learn. Parents are sending their kids off to learn at an earlier and earlier age.

Better late than never: It is never too late to learn anything, neither is it too early.

Many lecturers seem to talk to the overhead projector because the students are either not following them or daydreaming.

If you are thirsty for knowledge, avoid dry lecturers.

Do not underrate any simple skill. For all you know, it could turn out to be useful on the most unexpected occasion.

I prefer letters written by hand. They have this certain charm not obtainable by emails.

It is funny: words are made up of letters, but letters are made up of words.

Is there such a person as an honest liar? Yes, an honest liar is one who thinks he is being honest to himself when he lies to others.

In the name of liberty, how many heinous crimes have been committed?

Give me liberty or give me death. Fine, but absolute liberty never exists, for absolute liberty creates absolute chaos.

The one thing I will miss dearly when I retire is the library. Not only has it been part of me for a long time, but also the cost of good, new books has been skyrocketing.

How can you cheat life when there are no answers to life in any book?

I am pessimistic about the world, but I am optimistic about myself – especially now that I am getting older.

Someone has likened life to a telescope: an optimist looks into one end and a pessimist the other.

The images in a telescope are all virtual. Indeed, are we not all looking at virtual images almost all the time in life?

It is all right to be optimistic. However, to be over-optimistic about everything is to court trouble.

In a world of suffering, a little optimism is like a small candle in the dark.

No one owes you anything, you owe everyone a bit of your living – just think where your food and shelter came from.

A good painting is to be admired and not explained.

Painters do not normally make money, the art galleries and the auctioneers do.

I would rather be a parent in the nineteenth century than the twenty-first century.

Two wrongs certainly do not make one right, neither would two rights necessarily make one right.
A 'no' is a 'no'. Would a no 'no' make a 'yes'?

All this nonsense about the Y2K – what a joke the

whole thing was! Nobody gained anything except that the media, and their associates became richer.

What is so special about life, which begins with a cry and ends with a sigh?

Life assurance does not assure your longevity. All it does is to ensure your beneficiary gets a lump sum if nothing goes wrong with your death.

If I had a choice, I would choose a gentle light that illuminates my surrounding at night, rather than a dazzling glare that blinds me even in the day.

The darker the conspiracy, the faster it comes to light.

The darkest time of the day is the moment before dawn arrives.

Scientists have discovered that mice have genetic structures rather similar to human beings. Will anyone be surprised if they come up with a human with a mouse brain?

There is a limit to everything – no, not to the people who spread rumours.

Intelligence has its ceiling, but stupidity does not.

A drunkard says he is exercising his self-control to a certain limit – he does not exceed a bottle of liquor a day.

A little liquor now and then will often end up as more liquor now than then.

It's not that no one is listening; it's just that many people listen by their mouths.

He is a good listener – he either does not know what to say or he does not know what has been said.

All that glitters is not gold – of course, there are many artificial stones.

Life seems to come in three stages: learning, earning and meaning.

Logic is a double-edged sword; it works both ways – for or against.

The world is fast becoming dichotomised – the sellers and the consumers.

One simply cannot afford to be too serious when it comes to self-praising.

When you are successful, you are always self-made. When you fail, it is because of others.

If you love yourself, you will never want to harm yourself by doing stupid things.

It is not that difficult to know others, but to many people it is just impossible to know themselves.

You can try to keep many things to yourself for many years, but you may not keep your opinion about yourself for a day.

You can lose your money or property, but never lose your self-respect.

Some of us do not appear to be aware of our self-praising; somehow, many are certainly unaware of their self-deceiving.

There is only one word in the mind of almost

everyone every moment. That is *self*.

Keeping your self-control is virtuous under many circumstances. However, keeping your self-control all the time in all circumstances may not be that virtuous after all.

Keep your head cool when the surroundings are hot. Remain warm when things turn cool.

Other people may perish in their millions, but you can still keep cool. However, you will heat up at the very moment when your hand is cut.

As they get older, women will look around more and more, and the men less and less.

Which would be your choice: a short sparkling life or a long insipid one?

It is so easy to find sporting winners around. But try looking for a good loser!

Love means different things to different age groups: excitement to the young, friendship to the middle-aged, and interdependence to the old.

To live is to love, you just swap the I for an O.

Love is blind. No, not in this modern era, it comes with four big eyes.

To a fool, love can be wisdom; to a wise man, love may fast turn into folly.

Love is only powerful when it is still fresh. Somehow it seems to weaken by the year.

All love can be questionable, except parental love.

Love with an ulterior motive attached is not love, it is deception of the worst kind.

True love is not made up of two pairs of eyes gazing at each other; instead the pairs of eyes should gaze forward in the same direction.

To a man, love begins in his eyes; to a lady, love starts at her ears.

Is there any difference between sexual desire and love?

People used to say that man gives love for sex and woman gives sex for love. This does not seem to be correct nowadays, it could well be the other way round.

It was once the norm for people to fall in love first and get married after. Now it is cohabitation before love, to be followed by separation.

Why get married then when the divorce rate has soared to 50%?

Which is true – love at first sight, or love is blind? Both cannot happen simultaneously.

It might have been better to love after marriage then to get married after love.

Love between a man and a woman is the most inconsistent of all inconsistencies, for it can fade away so fast that it would be gone before both even realise it.

Of course love can be blind, otherwise how could it lead to a blank marriage?

Marriage can be an eye-opener, especially for those

blinded by love.

Happy is the person who marries the loved one; happier is the person who loves the one after marriage.

To a large extent, every lover is a gentle hypocrite.

He who does not write love letters has missed the fun of a lifetime.

All the world loves a lover, albeit only for a day or two.

The world has really become a global village, too small to take in another car in the parking lot.

You can have a passion for something, but never be over-passionate about it.

Money has become very powerful; it can buy everything except one's past.

How can you not believe in luck? How else can you explain the success of someone whom you think is less capable than you?

A very effective way of making your not so good friends feel uncomfortable is to tell them all the lucky things that have happened to you.

Why do people like magicians but avoid tricky people?

Do not be surprised to find countries (including the democratic ones) where the minority rules and the majority follows.

In the final analysis, man is the biggest freak of evolution or creation.

Men are less than interesting, women are no better

than fascinating.

Marriage is a wedlock, where three out of seven wed and four out of seven lock.

Divorce is so rampant that it makes marriage redundant.

Just because someone dies for a conviction, it does not necessarily make the conviction right.

Have we not gone too far into materialism, consumerism and tourism?

Mathematically speaking, a physicist is a mathematician. Physically speaking, a mathematician needs not be a physicist.

There is so much mathematics in physics that one wonders when is physics not mathematics.

A mathematician is someone who cannot be certain of what he is talking about; nor is he certain that what he is talking about is certainty.

It is strange that some people mean what they meant, some meant what they mean, and the rest do not mean what they meant.

Medical sciences are full of uncertainties. They are merely probabilities.

Girls have wonderful memories. They memorise all the wrong things you have done.

I am starting to lose my memories. The best cure is perhaps to forget I have had those memories.

People tend to have a short memory about things they

get, but they can remember for a very long time things they give.

How many of us would stop after making the first million? Chances are we would go for the second, the third or even the hundredth.

A life with too many secrets is an unhealthy and miserable life.

Someone said that science without religion is lame, and religion without science is blind. Maybe it should be science without religion is blind, and religion without science is more than lame.

Science is only a faith when religion starts losing flavour.

Knowledge need not come from school. What is the point of going to school when the teachers teach something you do not want to know, and you cannot learn from anybody things you want to know?

This is rather annoying: why are great men in history never great scholars?

Scandal has its share. It keeps many a gossip going.

When is an insult not an insult, when is a sarcasm a sarcasm?

Wise Sayings, or Just Empty Words

Never allow your weaknesses to tamper with your strengths.

Fulfilment of a talent requires a successful blending of motivation, perseverance, personality and opportunity. That is why so many talents remain dormant.

If you think you have already accomplished all you can in life, then you are as good as a piece of dead wood.

Talking without action is empty, yet how often we indulge in this useless activity.

The world would be a more beautiful place if only there were fewer dreamers than movers.

Knowledge/skills + action + sweat + diligence + luck = success.

Just having ideas is not enough; what we need is immediate and purposive action.

If you wait for insight and inspiration to drop by before you attempt to do anything, then you may end up in doing nothing.

Accept all adversities in life, because there is no way you can escape. The essence is to meet them with courage and tackle them the best you can. That is learning.

Good advice comes rarely. Most advice is either

something you already know or something you are not willing to heed.

When you need twice as long, and thrice as much effort to finish only half the job you would normally take, old age is beginning to set in.

Can age be just a number? It is if you act so, it is not if you think so.

As soon as you begin to come to terms with death, you have already crossed the threshold of old age.

When you start thinking about the wonderful things you have done while young, that is the time old age creeps in.

Judge not others, lest you want to be judged.

Do not look down on people whom you think are less capable than you. For all you know, these are the people who would come to your help in times of need.

For every finger you point at others, there are at least three fingers pointing at your own self simultaneously. (Haven't you heard that before?)

You need imagination to be creative; but you require action in order to accomplish.

Never impose your own idiosyncrasy on others, not even someone very close; for the simple reason that he or she is just not you.

Words are certainly mightier than the sword. A sword may injure or kill a person, but insulting and provocative words can bring nations to war.

Evolution must have played a trick on us: we have eyes only to look outward at somebody else's faults, but none to look inwards at our own inadequacies and weaknesses.

A killer argues that it is not his intention to shoot, his impulsive and murderous genetic make-up leaves him with no other choice. Who should be sentenced to death, the killer or his genes?

Once upon a time, ignorance could be blissful – not now anymore.

We are all pawns of the great game of probability. Life itself is a big gamble.

'No pain, no gain.' This used to be true, but it's not quite so nowadays. For many of us in the third world, it has been 'Great pain, no gain.'

It is not your fault if you trip and fall; but you are the only one to be blamed if you do not try to get up yourself.

Though having a positive and right attitude may not mean everything in life, the opposite is certainly the main cause of your downfall.

Attitude is the exact mirror image of your personality and character.

Strong belief and conviction have been the two main forces behind all civilisations.

The right belief promotes, the wrong belief destroys.

If you cannot have the right kind of belief, than do not believe in anything; for the wrong kind of belief can bring nothing but catastrophe.

There are many constants in nature. However, there is only one constant in life: that is the constant of variability, the constant of change.

Never assume that change is always for the better, very often it entices chaos.

In the name of progress, people want change – this unfortunately is a perpetual misconception.

In life's journey, we face many junctions that allow us to make choices. More often than not, the choices are not entirely ours, but those of our family, career and circumstances.

Interest is not commitment. You need not be committed if you are interested, but if you are committed, then surely you would have been interested.

If you do not know how to say the right thing at the right time and right moment, then don't say anything.

Some people believe they are straightforward and would want to speak their mind at all time. Do so by all means, but then learn how to choose the right platform.

How often do you say what you mean and mean what you say?

Provocative words are like sharp daggers. They not only always hurt, they sometimes kill.

Most communications are monologues. You say what you want to say, and I say what I want to tell. None would ever bother to listen or digest the content.

It is strange but true – a brilliant mind seldom comes with a sharp tongue.

Never equate courage with fearlessness. Courage comes from the successful overcoming of intense fears, one of which is fear of death.

New ideas + insight + commitment + courage + persistence = creativity.

Not all imaginations have creativity. But most creativity comes from a daring imagination.

Creativity means different things to different people. It is more of an art than science – it is the art of science.

You can never be creative if you fear criticism, ridicule and making mistakes – and most of all, if you fear making a fool of yourself.

How many of us can take criticism in our stride? This is because we always think we are a few notches above those who criticise us.

Is it not better to be dead than a live zombie?

Desire has two faces: one that will lead you to ruin and the other to glory. The only drawback is there will be far more ruins than glories.

Intense desire creates a powerful drive, and this may lead to catastrophe if the desire is of the undesirable kind.

Often the demarcation line between possibility and impossibility is very thin – the determining factors are the state of mind of the person and his determination.

Life without a dream is dry, a dream without making it happen in life is even worse.

Nowadays, diplomas and degrees come in every shade and in all kinds of colours. If you cannot prove yourself worthy of your job, your paper qualification is as good as useless, even if it is from a well-known institution.

If you think education is that expensive, why not try illiteracy.

Far too many people are willing to spend lavishly on food, cars and houses. Only a few less than stupid people would want to pay the same amount for education.

We are so immersed in the dull routine of our working life that we do not seem to have time to pause for a while and ask, 'What am I doing this for, anyway?'

No amount of beating will make a horse move, but a few gentle strokes and good gestures will send it racing through the field in no time.

You only need a few words of encouragement at the right time to see how a person can be changed overnight.

Why can't we replace torrents of abusive remarks by a few words of encouragement? Wouldn't life be more wonderful that way?

As if there is not enough suffering in life, why add salt to the wound again?

Hope is the rare ingredient that sustains life. Without hope, there is no life.

Be enthusiastic and passionate in what you do; otherwise, the road to success will be a long and tortuous one.

Beware of someone with bland talk – for half the time he is either lying or making up stories.

Two words starting with the letter 'p' are often associated with the 'p' of great pretenders. The first 'p' is politician, and the second 'p' is still politician.

If you cannot or do not know how to lead, then you may be a good follower. If you are neither a leader nor a follower, then try and learn to become an adviser.

Mass media can help to make you popular. The irony is that the more popular you become, the blinder the public – especially when your mediocrity is inflated out of proportion.

There is a price to pay for everything, indeed, everything under the sun.

Nothing smells sweeter than success. Success leads to success. Success led by success breeds further success.

There are no fixed criteria for gauging success in life. Most people would judge by wealth, power, status and fame. Nonetheless, others would look at academic or non-academic excellence, health, happiness, a good spouse and nice children, right thinking and right behaviour, a substantial publication, a useful discovery and invention, a beneficial contribution to mankind in one way or other, as well as deep spiritual and religious satisfaction.

Do we not build our success on our failures? How many of us can have achievements without going through a series of errors?

Great credit should be given to those who dare to try what others dare not, never mind if they fail repeatedly.

Who wants failure? Yet how many would appreciate the fact that failure is the mother of success. (Somebody said this before.)

Forgiveness is the main course of life's curriculum. The assignment is difficult, the exam is even tougher.

If everyone only looks for friends who are better off or more capable, then who will befriend the less than mediocre ones?

One is often judged by the friend(s) one has. There may be exceptional cases, though.

A miser who saves every cent may not be happy. But the miser who saves every friendship is the happiest person on earth.

Good friends are hard to come by, and few. Treasure them by all means, for the great majority of people you know are either acquaintances (including relatives) or casual business customers (including colleagues).

The sweetest accomplishment is one when you are only aware of it after being congratulated by a stranger.

Fear not the future or the unknown. You will know

how to cross the bridge only when you reach it. (Did you say that before?)

The future belongs to people who have hope, courage and conviction.

The more one gives, the more one has. This is not illogical when what one gives are love and kindness.

Many people seem to know that happiness comes from giving and not taking. Unfortunately, knowing is one thing, practising is another.

Everyone has something to give in life, even the poorest of the poor. Indeed, the poor can offer kindness, which the rich appear to lack.

Still Trying to Understand Religion by Asking Questions

1. Does religion mean tranquillity or unsettledness, sanity or madness, compassion or cruelty, peace or war, reality or miracle, holiness or immorality, sincerity or deception, faith or myth, friendship or persecution, sublimation or horror, reverence or killing?

2. Or is religion the sum total of all the characteristics mentioned in question one?

3. How often has religion been manipulated to become the means of a political end?

4. Is religion basically ritualistic – focussed on worship, devotion and prayer?

5. Is it not that the religious concept of soul happens to be the reflection of humans' selfish and futile craving for eternal life?

6. Does religion not promise a blissful life in heaven because life on earth is either unbearable or tortuous, with endless suffering?

7. Why should religion centre on the elusive idea of an inaccessible world of gods, angels, devils and the like, to indoctrinate the minds of the people?

8. Supernatural power of an almighty 'being' seems to

be the denominator of all religions. Does this imply that humans have been so helpless throughout recorded history that we must cling desperately to an invisible 'being'?

9. Or the need for religion is purely psychological, the very weakness of humans who fear for their lives and their unpredictable day-to-day existence?

10. Or the need for religion is wholly spiritual, reflecting the need to hold onto the precarious consciousness that seems to be the unique possession of humans?

11. Is religion the sole product of emotion rather than intelligent and logical reasoning?

12. Was religion created to pacify human anxiety and insecurity? To cope with the uncontrollable forces of death and despair, ignorance and injustice?

13. Or was religion formed as a result of human endeavour to satisfy personal ego, sexual expression, self-esteem and individual deprivation of some kind?

14. In this new millennium of super technology and science, do we still need religion? Why? Why not?

Still Trying to Fathom the Meaning of Life

1. Are justice and fairness two concepts that are only applicable to humans? In other words, do animals think (!) or care about justice and fairness at all?

2. We use our own yardstick to measure right and wrong, justice and injustice, morality and immorality, depending on the benchmark arbitrarily set up by different groups of people and community.

3. Or is it true that life is meant to be like what it has been all the time, throughout the history of mankind? Is life never meant to be understood by the product of evolution itself (because, otherwise, we would not be around in the first place). So what is the use of searching for the meaning of life in the first place? It is absurd and preposterous.

4. Do not ask why some are much more fortunate than others. Do not even point a finger at the rich and the powerful and question their legitimacy. They are what they are despite the rest. Why? Because that is what it is. Stupid questions deserve idiotic answers.

5. Do not ask why you were born in a poor or low-caste family. Never ask why you miss the womb of a wealthy, highly intelligent or powerful mother. For, do not forget that if everyone were to have super-parents, they would all have a super-life. But if everyone lead a super-life, then everyone would be the same, and no

one would know they were already living a super-life. Would they not then want to aim for an *ultra* super-life, just to be a notch better than others?

6. Do you not see that most human problems are man-made and man-imagined?

7. By virtue of our very existence and consciousness, we began to think a few thousand years ago. And by the freak gift of evolution that enabled us to think, we started the first step of creating endless problems for ourselves. Are we ever satisfied, or can we be?

8. We have practically no satisfactory answers for most encounters in life. Worst of all we fear death, and we frantically seek help to prolong our very 'being' in this world. We created the concept of soul, we invented heaven in the name of religion simply because we wanted an afterlife, a more blissful life of perpetual happiness in the kingdom of god(s). Are we not cheating ourselves?

9. We are all blurred (some partially, others completely) by our insatiable desire for everything. We want this, we want that, if we can – everybody wants everything. But how can we be so blind as to be totally unable to see the futility and impossibility of this? Are we moronic, idiosyncratic, ignorant or what? Nonetheless, everyone thinks they are smart, at least smarter than their neighbours. Are they not?

10. Ask no more. Many valuable lives have been wasted in trying to look for solutions to these answers, and these so-called thinkers or philosophers die sad and in agony. Who knows what has happened to them?

Heaven knows if they are in heaven. So take a break and ask no more.

Just a Thought

Success is an elusive thing. It is relative and has a different benchmark for different people. What you look for in life determines your kind of expectation, which in turn measures your level of success. Below are some 'definitions' of success:

Success is when you pile up lots of money, never mind how the money is made.

Success is when you marry someone whom you have been dreaming of.

Success is when you earn your first Diploma or Degree, no matter how bogus it is.

Success is when you think you have brought up your family through thick and thin.

Success is when you have had a healthy, long and 'eventful' life.

Success is when you become famous and popular, irrespective of the means you employ to make it.

Success is when you taste the sweetness of power. Who cares how many bodies you have had stepped on?

Success is when you make a discovery or invent something, regardless of it benefiting anybody or not.

Success is when you are given the due recognition of your lifelong work by people, how many of them is not important.

Success is when you watch your grown-up children, educated and trained to become useful citizens.

Success is when you know your name will be down in history, no matter if it is for good or for bad.

Success is when you think you are successful, ignoring completely what other people may opine.

Success is when you are surrounded by your cronies, whose flatteries and false smiles become your daily subsistence.

…and so on and so on…

So, it is not that difficult to be successful in life after all. You lower your expectations a bit, work a bit harder, make your skin somewhat thicker, get ready to take advantage of others, hunt for the right godfather or godmother, and are always prepared to lie and deceive to move further up. Of course, there is a common element along the line for everyone – the all important element of luck.

The unsuccessful ones blame their fate. They equate fate to having no luck, and complain that the goddess of fortune never visits them. But why worry about success at all? Why choose another's yardstick as the criterion of your success? Isn't a simple and peaceful life a success too?

To me, as long as one lives an honest life, harm no one, betray none, cheat nobody and be virtuous and upright, that itself is a success. Come to think of it, how many people can make this grade? Certainly you can argue that all these standards may be relative. Yes, you are right. We all have different benchmarks for everything in life; what else is not relative?

Who is What?

While thinking about human interactions and the livelihood of all the multitudes of people, it occurs to me that our concepts of living and perceptions of the nature of mankind are quite distorted. We seem to have attached wrong conventional meanings to a string of words which should have meant otherwise. The following are examples:

Who is rich? Someone who shares what he has with others, someone who gives but does not take.

Who is powerful? Someone who works for the good and welfare of others, the one who champions the rights of the dispossessed.

Who is strong? Someone who knows how to contain his fear and control his inner rage, the one who helps the weak.

Who is wise? Someone who learns from others and is humble.

Who is honourable? Someone who honours all his fellow beings.

Who is noble? Someone who has nothing but compassion.

Who is sagely? Someone who practises the good deeds he preaches.

Who is virtuous? Someone who lives with dignity and honesty.

Who is poor? Someone who accumulates wealth and selfish possessions.

Who is ignorant? Someone who does not know the teachings of the sages.

Who is innocent? Someone who was born a minute ago.

Who is knowledgeable? Someone who knows he is not knowledgeable.

Who is happy? Someone who understands the transience of life.

Who is wealthy? Someone who owes no one and is owed by none.

Who is healthy? Someone who refrains from sensual activities, excessive food and toxic drinks; the one who does not indulge in bodily pleasure.

Who is respectable? Someone who respects others, the one who suffers for the welfare of others.

Who is brave? Someone who faces death with calm, the one who tolerates the intolerable.

Who is foolish? Someone who clings dearly to every possession.

Who is idiotic? Someone who thinks the world owes him a living.

Who is pathetic? Someone who believes he was born to be great.

Who is great? Someone who thinks with humility and cares for others, the one who is reticent and at peace with himself.

Who is blind? Someone who can see himself but not others.

Who is pitiable? Someone who lies and steals but does not blush; the one who hurts others but pretends to repent.

Who is kind? Someone who does not know hatred, and does not have the words envy and jealousy in his vocabulary.

Who is generous? Someone who loves every other human being.

Who is enlightened? Someone who fully grasps the true meaning of impermanence of life.

Some Reflections

When I was a child in my small hometown along the East Coast of Malaya, my house always had our front or back door (or both doors) left open during the daytime. This also applied to many of my neighbours.

In those days, we could walk in the front door and out of the back door of our neighbours' houses without anyone raising an eyebrow.

In those good old days, if any of my neighbours was having tea or coffee and anyone happened to drop in, he or she, young or old, would certainly be offered a cup too.

Those were the days when hospitality was a norm. No one would ask you to pay, or reciprocate the hospitality.

That was a time when one did not have to make an appointment to visit anybody's home at any hour of the day or night.

The neighbours were prompt to offer help at all times. If you were on an urgent errand and had to leave the house for a few hours, you just notified them and they would be quick to respond by looking after your children and your house.

Theft was practically unheard of in the small town and robbery was unknown. Perhaps all of us were too poor to attract any thief or robber.

Our Malay neighbours a short distance away would

not latch their doors either. On stepping into any of their houses, you would be their instant guest.

Somehow, the Chinese and Malays were closer and more friendly than they are today. Smiling faces were everywhere.

There were then very few motor vehicles. You could play on the streets at any time without fear of being run down by a car.

Bicycles were more common, they were the main mode of transportation.

Imagine a young boy of nine or ten riding an oversized bicycle. He would have one leg on the left pedal and cross the other leg under the bar to the right pedal. One slight push from him, and the bicycle would wobble all over the street.

Falling down and getting hurt on the kneecaps while learning to ride a bicycle was a common thing. No fear, he would wipe off the blood, apply some saliva on the wound, ignore the pain and went on with the bicycle again in no time.

My hometown has since developed beyond recognition. The old wooden houses have disappeared, the trees by the roadside have long been chopped down, and the children's playing fields could not be traced. It is not the place I used to know; I have lost my hometown, and I'm not sure for better or worse.

Why Should it be Me?

Outside the capital city of Malaya, Kuala Lumpur, in the later part of 1950s, there were a number of lakes. These were the remnants of tin mining and the results of reckless excavation of tin ore. The dredging went hundreds of feet deep, while the diameters of the man-made cavities can be as wide as a quarter of a mile. When it was found to be less and less profitable to dig further in, the mines were just abandoned. Years of rainfall gradually filled them up to make lakes. These lakes appeared to be shallow, but they were deceptively deep.

Near the edge of one of these lakes were sheds built in haste to house a sizable number of Chinese families. Most of them moved in from New Villages in other parts of Selangor State and Perak State. The New Villages were specially established in the late 1940s and early 1950s by the British government during the communist insurgency after WWII. The purpose was to contain the suspected Chinese communist sympathisers and to fence them in to restrict their movement. As the villagers became poorer and poorer, they fled to the more prosperous city to look for jobs.

Siew Cheng was a mother in her late thirties. Her labourer husband and three children were staying with her in one of the sheds near a lake. The eldest was a teenage daughter, and the two younger sons were twelve and ten years old. None of the children went to school, for the nearest primary school was some four miles away, and all secondary schools were in the city, fifteen miles as the crow flew. Cheng's husband rarely came home; he worked as a night guard in one of the small factories on the other side of the city. She herself was an odd-job woman; half her time was spent earning a tiny daily wage, and the other half wasted in moving about looking for job. The daughter was employed as a part-time stay-in babysitter, and the two boys were left either idling their time at home or loitering in the nearby hills and fields. Sometimes, the elder brother would use a Y-shaped elastic band to shoot at birds or bring down fruit from trees. The younger one would imitate the action at every possible opportunity.

Cheng did not quite mind the boys roaming in the hills, what she feared most was the lake. None of the family knew how to swim and that was all the more reason for stopping the boys from dipping in the lake.

Now you two listen carefully. Never ever go near the lake. The water may appear shallow, but we do not really know how deep it may be because it is rather muddy. Don't ever let me catch any one of you splashing water at the edge of the lake. I will punish you severely.

How many times had Cheng warned her boys, and the boys would quietly nod their heads. As usual, after preparing some porridge – enough to feed the boys for the day – Cheng would light a joss stick and bow in front of the family guardian deity, and then pray to the Goddess of Mercy before leaving the house early in the morning every day, seven days a week.

It was a rather unusual hot day. The air was humid. The noon sun was quick to show its radiating power, forcing everyone walking under it to sweat profusely. Inside the shed, where the air could be suffocating, it was no better. It would not be the right day to hike in the fields, or forests nearby either. Finding nothing else better to do, the boys decided to cool themselves down a bit in the lake. That was not the first time they were ever by the lake side. For despite the constant warning of their mother, they had wet themselves in the lake water a good number of times. They knew that their shorts would dry long before their mother's return, and she would believe them when they denied they had been near the lake.

At first they played by the water's edge, then they became a bit more adventurous, moving into deeper water. The younger one was a bit reluctant at first, but seeing the elder brother enjoying himself immersing in the deeper water, he was tempted to follow suit. Both of them seemed to have found a new way to have fun, and were hardly aware that the younger brother was already shorter than the depth of the water. They had never learned to swim, let alone in such a depth of water. Before the elder boy sensed the danger and yelled to his brother to move ashore, the younger one was nowhere to be seen. A sudden coldness ran through his spine; he knew what could have happened, and he truly panicked.

He wanted to shout for help, but no sound came out from his wide-open mouth. In fact, even if he could yell to burst his lungs, nobody would be around to hear him. He struggled and dashed toward the shore, straining his eyes hard, hoping to catch a glimpse of his younger brother. There was no sign of another human being. Now he was really scared, scared stiff. He wanted to run, but his legs simply refused to move. Minutes went by, and still no sign of his younger brother. He made a final effort and used all his energy to pull his legs along. He headed for his shed. He could not shout anymore, all he knew was that cold beads of sweat were oozing out all over his body. He was exhausted and collapsed on the earthen floor on reaching the shed…

He must have slept for quite some time, for when he came to, it was already dusk. He forgot about his hunger, for he knew that his mother would return very soon. He started crying, blaming himself for taking his brother to the lake and not being able to save him when he was in trouble. He kept on banging his fist on the floor, without knowing any pain. He was absolutely numb, the only thing that occupied his head was how to tell his mother of the accident – that he had lost his brother. He was in a state of utter despair.

There were sounds of hurried foot steps getting closer. His mother appeared.

What on earth is happening to you? Why are you sitting on the floor? And look at your eyes, did you have a fight with someone? Cheng pumped a series of questions at her elder son. Then she realised that the younger son was not around.

Where is your younger brother? quizzed Cheng. And when she saw him bursting into tears and crying louder, Cheng sensed something had gone awfully wrong.

Where is your brother? Where did he go? What has happened? She was almost yelling away. Then a dark shadow crossed her mind.

Did your brother go to the lake? Tell me, did he? Cheng was almost hysterical. Without waiting for the son's answer, she dashed straight to the lake, tripping over a stone on her way.

Where are you, my precious son? Come back to me wherever you are!

She kept on yelling over the lake, and walked to and fro along the shore. There was no answer, the only sound was from the insects nearby. Her shrieking voice attracted some neighbours, and they all knew what had happened. A few housewives came and tried to comfort Cheng. But Cheng continued shrieking at the top of her voice. Seeing that there was not much they could do to help, the women left one by one, for they had their own urgent matters to attend to.

Cheng knelt down by the shore, surrounded by complete darkness. A small dark figure crept towards her – the elder brother too knelt beside his grieving mother.

Oh, Kuan-yin, my Goddess of Mercy. Why did you not save my child? Isn't that the reason I pray to you every morning? What have I done wrong to be fated this way? Oh, god of the heavens, if you really wanted to take away a life from my family, why didn't you pick me? Why did you choose my youngest child instead? That is not fair, not fair! Why should I be the one suffering from all fate? Why should it be me?... Cheng wailed and wailed, her voice got softer and softer until it disappeared into the darkness of the cruel night.

The only sound around was the numerous noises made by the unknown insects and small animals in the fields, in the forests and in the hills… Were they sympathising with Cheng over the untimely and tragic loss of her son? Or were they singing the tunes they had sung for millions of years? The passing away of a human being had no relevance to them, or for that matter to anybody else, except Cheng's family…

Index

www.ingramcontent.com/pod-product-compliance
Lightning Source LLC
Chambersburg PA
CBHW051447250726
48655CB00001B/278